PATIENTS, PATIENCE

AND THE TALKING CURE

PATIENTS, PATIENCE AND THE TALKING CURE

A Week in the Mind of a Psychotherapist

Mary Davis, MD

IPBOOKS.net
International Psychoanalytic Books

New York • http://www.IPBooks.net

Published by International Psychoanalytic Books (IPBooks)
Queens, NY
Online at www.IPBooks.net

Book design and formatting services by Self-Publishing Lab

Front cover design by Kathy Kovacic, BlackthornStudio.com

ISBN: 978-1-949093-23-0

Contents

Foreword

D.W. Winnicott once wrote that maturation *"requires and depends on the quality of the facilitating environment"* (Winnicott 1960; italics in original); in her book, Mary Davis welcomes us into her consulting room, and into her environment. Chronicling a week in her life as a psychiatrist/psychoanalyst, or psychoanalyst/psychiatrist, Dr. Davis invites us to walk through her office door, into the machinations of her mind and her work. In a candid, clear, unguarded and genuine manner, we encounter her patients as she encounters them, coffee in hand, coming together, to be and make some sense together. In the true Winnicottian sense, the environment of the book, of Dr. Davis' story, includes not just the details of construction, the office suite, the objects that occupy the space, and the colors on the walls, but the ambiance, body language, physical attributes and attire of the cast of characters, the tones and nuances of the interactions as Dr. Davis perceives them.

Early on we know that Winnicott occupies an organizing force in Dr. Davis' thinking and action. Those already familiar with Winnicott's work will immediately feel at ease, and those who are not will likely gain an appreciation for his kind, bold, collaborative and thoughtful clinical approach, and want to read more first-hand after finishing this book. A master integrationist, Winnicott challenged the status quo of his training and of the clinical ethos of his time, relying on a background in pediatrics and attention to the complex nuances of family life and major life transitions to create space for the real world and real relationships in his clinical work. Dr. Davis also works with individuals across the lifespan, with a balance of playfulness and seriousness. She creates a holding space that people can rely on, one that is true to herself and to the work.

Dr. Davis' descriptions of assessment, process, and intervention, like those of her teacher, are clear, descriptive, and often deceptively simple or straightforward. At first glance, her comfortable prose may mask nuance and depth. As she walks us through her door and down her hall into her space, pointing out the furniture and decor and providing a historical context for why the space is how it is, and disclosing the thoughts and intentions behind her decorative choices, it is easy to feel like one is walking beside her, and really seeing what it is like to be in her space. Of course we are seeing things through her lens, which illuminates what she selects for our attention, and what we see takes shape in our minds based on our own lenses, paralleling her experience of bearing witness to much more than her patients reveal anywhere else, while only seeing so much. A patient cleverly notes that her office provides "things to look at when you need distraction …but everything can mean whatever you need it to mean." Another notices a "new" object that has been in the same place for a decade. While reading, I could not help but think about my own office spaces, seeing them now as my patients might, and noticing things in my mind's eye about my patients that I had not quite realized before. Anything and everything, from the unintentional office features left over from previous occupants to the carefully selected personal photograph, can barely register or can serve to reveal important aspects of a person's subjective experience.

Dr. Davis makes home visits, sits in silence, works therapeutically once, twice, three or four times a week; she does analysis on the couch, or patients sit up; she works Saturdays and writes notes during sessions and reports on adolescent offenders. People come with worry, fear, loneliness, confusion, anger, hurt, sadness, joy, relief, hypervigilance, and they may or may not want to be there. Teaching and supervision happens *in situ* or via online platform with students in China, and together they grapple with distance and differences.

This is a full and varied work week, likely a range of activities that would surprise the non-clinician and aspiring clinician, and yet it all makes sense as Dr. Davis explains it, and is a view of (typical?) private-practice life obscured to most. Much of training — and contemporary clinical research — occurs in settings that do not resemble the work of professionals in the world. On graduation, psychiatrists, psychologists and social workers have learned in hospital and clinic settings, from attending and senior clinicians who have knowledge and expertise, but they may not have stepped outside those clinical milieus. The trained clinician/analyst will note how Dr. Davis' account runs counter to professional norms, particularly relative to many foundational psychoanalytic and psychological communities in this country, who hold the identity and thinking of the analyst as things to be hidden from view, not to be considered along with the real, lived realities of the patient. Thus Dr. Davis' invitation into her office, and into her mind, takes a page from those trailblazers before her, and represents a challenge to standard clinical reading, writing, and training.

Today's aspiring clinicians are faced with a staggering array of treatments and treatment orientations, that increasingly mean rules and guidelines for what intervention is supposed to be applied to a given ailment. With the proliferation and popularity of manualized treatments and supposed evidence-based treatments (EBTs), we come to exist in a medicalized world of symptoms that have corresponding treatments independent of contextualizing factors. The psychiatry residents and psychology doctoral students I encounter in my work are often master diagnosticians, and can readily identify signs and symptoms, and articulate a clear diagnostic rationale. Some can rely on a framework or orientation for articulating a clinical picture, paying attention to personality or character structure while looking beyond the immediate presentation to the impact of circumstance. A few exceptional ones can speak knowledgeably about the ways in which given familial, social, cultural, economic and generational factors interact; can consider the ways in which maladaptive perceptions/thoughts/behaviors are paradoxically derivative of adaptive mechanisms; and can recognize their own role or influence in the process. Weaving theory, reflection, and experience critically throughout the description of her week's work, Dr. Davis will inspire the beginning clinician to seek more learning than what is typically offered, and excite the seasoned clinician to think anew about learned practices and ingrained tendencies.

What kind of therapy is this, some readers will ask. It is not CBT (cognitive behavioral therapy) or IPT (interpersonal psychotherapy) or anything manualized; it is not psychoanalysis as it is portrayed in mainstream or academic writing, or as it is represented in institute training. And yet it is unapologetically psychodynamic, psychoanalytic, based in sound clinical theory and research. It is also technical, experiential, and disciplined. And yet flexible — the work meets patients where they are, in very individual and also disciplined ways, as Dr. Davis elucidates throughout. It is based on an understanding of how information is processed, how memory works, how development proceeds across the lifespan, how resilience co-exists with maladaptive ways of thinking, perceiving and experiencing. Good clinicians are the ones persistently growing, learning, expanding and questioning, no matter how skilled and experienced. It is important for those at the beginning and middle (and ends!) of their careers to be reminded of the need to keep learning. While much of the work that Dr. Davis references is grounded in American Ego Psychology and British object-relations schools, she practices from a two-person psychoanalytic perspective. This is also importantly revealing, and reflects much of my own experience working within different systems and institutional frames: No matter the (theoretical) starting point, if done 'right' the work ends up looking and sounding similar.

Dr. Davis and her patients humanize symptoms and syndromes, demonstrating the challenges inherent in giving up clearly problematic modes of being. As we witness the struggle to make sense of unfulfilling relationships, repetitive self-sabotage, isolation, under-performance, and low self-worth, with Dr. Davis noting reasons for offering or avoiding various insights and directives, it is obvious why standardized, directive, behaviorally-oriented approaches often fail to elicit lasting results, and why patients may comply with instructions to please their therapists, who in turn offer reassurance, only to see their patients experience disappointment maybe with a dose of shame.

Starting from moments in the clinical encounter, and then stepping back to consider theory, technique, missteps, clinical goals of both patient and therapist, competition between goals/wishes and reality, Dr. Davis takes on some of the key questions that arise for any clinician at any time of their career. She addresses neutrality and self-disclosure, in a world where so much is revealed and available for scrutiny, and the patient whose trust has been damaged by prior malpractice. She takes us through the struggle to stay focused and engaged with certain people, and the power and importance of seeing things through, not rushing to speak/solve/understand, which seems particularly important in today's culture of immediacy and an increasingly entrenched insistence on instant gratification/ instant solutions. She shows a willingness to be seen and known, but within clear limits and parameters that still allow for fantasy and not-knowing, and to remain rooted in what makes clinical sense for the patient.

In multiple ways, this book mirrors the therapeutic process, whether psychoanalysis, psychotherapy or medication management, which is at once obvious and obscure; shared, individual, and co-constructed; explicit and private. We see what Dr. Davis chooses to show us, and while she makes explicit aspects of her process and reasoning, there is no doubt much that we do not get shown. That remainder we are left to create in our minds, in ways that are deeply satisfying while illuminating how much is left to be considered, known, or understood. We leave with some answers (to questions maybe we did not realize we were asking) and a lot of musings, considerations and unfinished business. It is a gift to witness Dr. Davis' curiosity and questions, her grappling with making sense of and understanding her patients; and their experience--with her and of her—is not something we often have the opportunity to observe, especially at this stage in a career.

The expert is always learning! And working towards improvement. Listening is powerful; being with another who is listening, wondering, and caring from a place of authenticity and non-judgment is powerful, as Dr. Davis shows/reminds us again and again.

Inga Blom, PhD

Licensed Clinical Psychologist

INTRODUCTION

Many years ago I saw a patient in my psychiatric office who was looking for help with her overwhelming anxiety about driving; she had been in an auto accident and was afraid to drive, but had to drive to keep her job. She wanted medication to stop the anxiety, and she didn't expect much else. She finally ended up coming five times a week for seven years of a psychoanalysis. About two years into her analysis, I reminded her that initially she had wanted only medication, and asked what had changed. She thought for a minute and then said, "You listened. And I wanted more of it."

That's what I do—I listen—and this book is about how I listen, and how being listened to can change lives.

I did not intend to spend my professional life as a psychoanalyst; I stumbled into it. When I was about twelve, I wanted to be a doctor, and I have never changed my mind. I didn't particularly want to be a psychiatrist, though, and I'm not even sure I knew what a psychiatrist was. When I started medical school, I intended to be a family doctor, who saved everybody and was loved by everybody—Marcus Welby, for fans of classic TV. In medical school, I discovered that most of the specialties were not especially exciting to me, although almost anything can be interesting if you learn enough to get into the intricacies and puzzles of the field. I also discovered that primary care physicians don't have a lot of time with their patients: for two months I worked with a family doctor who made hospital rounds at 7:00 a.m. and again at 7:00 p.m., and for the rest of the day never spent longer than ten minutes with any one patient. I didn't want that. I wanted to be able to know my patients more thoroughly. In my exposure to psychiatry, I had the opportunity to spend time with some of my patients, listening to them talk about what they needed help with. That was fascinating to me, so I chose psychiatry as my specialty.

The curriculum of the medical school I attended did not focus much on psychotherapy in the introduction to psychiatry, and included nothing at all about psychoanalysis. Instead, it leaned heavily on physical treatments—medication, electroconvulsive therapy—and as far as I knew that was what all psychiatrists did. Once I had decided on psychiatry, I was drawn even more strongly to child psychiatry. At the time, and for many years, I could not have told you what the attraction was. Now I know that child psychiatrists tend to be more flexible in dealing with their patients; they are more aware of all the ways children (and adults too) communicate without using words; and they are more aware of how developmental steps in children (such as learning to walk, read, make good decisions about friends) are continuous with developmental steps in adults (decisions about job choices, life partners, managing finances).

So I became a psychiatrist. In residency training, where you learn about the specialty you choose, I learned how to use medications. I learned how to talk with and listen to people who were psychotic (out of touch with reality), or just very confused; I learned a little bit about families and how an individual's emotional problems affect and are affected by his or her family. I learned something about psychotherapy, but my training focused on shorter-term therapies and problem solving, rather than the sorts of therapies that try to understand the meaning of behaviors. In child psychiatry we worked with family therapy, exploring how families contribute to the problems in the individual.

I was enthralled by the search for underlying patterns of connection between feelings and behavior.

At the University of Cincinnati, where I went for my child psychiatric fellowship (after three years of general psychiatry training), there was a strong emphasis on individual psychotherapy, psychodynamic understanding (the way that unconscious thoughts and feelings, as well as past history, shape behavior), and psychoanalytic thinking. I learned to listen not only to *what* people told me, but *how* they told me; I learned to hear beyond the words and see below the surface behaviors. And I learned to help my patients make their lives less painful. I was hooked. By the end of two years in Cincinnati, I was planning to become an analyst—even further, a child psychoanalyst, working with children, adolescents, and adults—to find ways of helping with psychological problems that did not rely primarily on medications. I've never regretted that choice.

The Effectiveness of Psychoanalytic Psychotherapy

When I began this book, I wanted to write about the choice I made at the beginning of my career to do psychoanalytic psychotherapy and psychoanalysis: why I believe this type of therapy works well, and why it has advantages for some people that medication and other more structured forms of therapy do not have. There is a widespread perception that psychoanalysis and psychoanalytic psychotherapy are outmoded and ineffective, and in the last fifteen years or so an academic emphasis on "evidence-based therapy" has often referred to psychoanalytic psychotherapy as if there is little or no evidence for its effectiveness. In fact, the power of psychoanalytic psychotherapy has been well established in recent research.

In 2015, Zimmerman et al examined the efficacy of psychoanalytic treatment and psychodynamic treatment in major depression, comparing specifically psychoanalytic therapy with psychodynamic therapy and cognitive-behavioral therapy (CBT, a popular current treatment described below). The study found that people who were involved in psychoanalytic therapy reported having fewer interpersonal problems, treated themselves in a more caring fashion immediately after treatment, and tended to improve in depressive symptoms and interpersonal problems over a three-year follow-up compared with patients receiving psychodynamic therapy or CBT (Masur 2018). The changes following treatment were found to be driven mostly by exploration of the patient's fantasy life and discussions of the patient's early memories. Masur notes that this is the "first evidence that intensive psychodynamic treatments are effective not only because they are intensive but also because they are psychoanalytic."

This is not the only research that supports the power of psychoanalytic psychotherapy (Freedman et al; Kernberg et al; Leichsenring; Clarkin et al; De Maat et al), but most people will never see that evidence, and, in this book, I am not addressing that. I believe that if people had a clear sense of what this type of therapy involved, they would value psychoanalytic ways of working. They might be glad for an opportunity to follow what goes on in the mind of an analyst as she struggles to find her way in the complexities of the lives of others.

Psychoanalysis and psychoanalytic therapies focus on recognizing unconscious as well as conscious feelings, thoughts, and motivations, and on understanding how those elements drive our conscious behaviors. They differ from behavior therapy, which views human behavior as shaped and reinforced by rewards from the surrounding environment (for instance, we go to work because we get a paycheck). Treatment with behavior therapy deals primarily with what people *do*, using a *stimulus-response* model of behavior with concrete rewards to reinforce desired behaviors; for example, giving your dog treats to teach him to sit on command. Psychoanalytic therapies also differ from cognitive therapy, which deals primarily with what people *think consciously* about their behaviors. Cognitive behavior therapy, a popular form of therapy today, assumes that a person's mood is directly related to his or her patterns of thought, and CBT interventions focus on helping people change how they think. For instance, CBT identifies counterproductive "thinking errors," such as a belief that if you lost your job you must be a loser and no good. The CBT therapist challenges those thinking errors and attempts to help the patent establish new ways of thinking about himself and his life circumstances.

Analytic psychotherapy will identify and challenge these distorted beliefs and patterns of thought, but with more focus on the emotions that accompany them. In analytic therapy, we believe that the mistaken beliefs made sense at some point in the patient's life, and that it helps to understand the age and the emotional context in which the mistaken beliefs made sense. One example would be a woman whose father was never at home and only at work, and so she learned to join him in his work to get his attention. This woman, as an adult, may not allow herself to have any personal life outside her own work because work is where "important" things happen. In analytic psychotherapy, we look at the ways in which patterns of behavior established in the past continue to occur in the present, even when they are no longer appropriate to the current emotional context of the patient. When people recognize the reflexive patterns of behavior from the past and see how they no longer fit the present situation, it becomes easier to interrupt those reflexive reactions in the present.

Research has also addressed the issue of how psychoanalytic psychotherapy differs from other forms of psychotherapy, such as CBT (which many people erroneously believe to be the only form of therapy that is "proven" to be effective). In a review of the literature comparing types of psychotherapy, Blagys and Hilsenroth (2000, in Masur 2018) identified seven interventions that distinguish psychodynamic and interpersonal therapy from CBT:

- focus on affect (emotional responses observed by others) and the expression of emotions
- exploration of a patient's attempts to avoid topics or engage in activities that hinder the progress of therapy (exploration of "resistance")
- identification of patterns in patients' actions, thoughts, feelings, experiences, and relationships
- emphasis on past experiences
- focus on patients' interpersonal experiences
- emphasis on the therapeutic relationship (the "transference"; see below)
- exploration of patients' wishes, dreams, or fantasies

This research makes it clear that behavior therapy, CBT, and other forms of therapy have been helpful to many people and have a valuable place in mental health treatment. Psychoanalytically informed treatment is also valuable, and for some people is more valuable than the shorter, more specifically behavior- or problem-focused therapies. Some people keep making the same mistakes over and over, like the woman who gets involved repeatedly with abusive men, leaving each in turn only to get involved with another abuser. They may need something different than treatments that focus on the problem behaviors; they need a treatment that will help them understand why they continue the problem behaviors and what role those behaviors play in their lives. For these individuals, therapies that are founded on psychoanalytic understandings about human behavior, what drives human behavior, and how people communicate unconsciously can be profoundly helpful.

The Power of Listening

Sometimes, just being listened to can be healing. As I struggled with how to show what I have learned in thirty-five years of practice about the power of psychoanalytic therapy, I remembered the patient who told me that she was "realizing the power of being able to be here, letting myself feel and think whatever's coming to mind." I also remembered the woman who stayed for seven years of psychoanalysis because she "wanted more" of my listening.

Listening to my patients has taught me that being listened to and learning to reflect on what is heard can be transformative. As I listen to what my patients tell me, and reflect with them on what I have heard from them, they learn to listen to themselves. As they do so, they learn about the origins of the unhappiness that brought them to treatment, and they learn to manage the pain that is a part of living. They become less likely to sabotage themselves as they go through their daily lives and more able to enjoy the good things in their lives.

I spend my working life trying to know others and helping them to know themselves. In the process, as an inevitable part of the process, I learn to know myself. Freud (1937) told us "that the analytic relationship is based on a love of truth—that is, on a recognition of reality." As I sit with and listen to my patients learn to recognize their own internal realities, we each find truths that we can build on for our futures.

The listening that uncovers those truths takes several different forms for me. Some patients I see only for medication, and they are in psychotherapy with another mental health professional. With those people, I listen mostly for information about symptoms of depression, anxiety, or whatever other symptoms the medication is targeting. I also listen for complaints about side effects, or comments that suggest the medication may be having negative effects. Even when I am primarily focused on the medication, however, I listen for information about life events, particular stresses, or what may have changed in the patient's life. One of the difficulties in this work is determining whether a patient feels less depressed, for instance, because the medication is working for him, or whether he feels better because he got a promotion and is more hopeful about the future. Distinguishing medication effects from reactions to life events is always a source of uncertainty.

Psychoanalytic Psychotherapy

The second type of listening I do is in psychoanalytic psychotherapy, with people I am seeing once or twice a week or less. With these patients, my focus is on both current reality and on unconscious content, the underlying thoughts and feelings that drive our behaviors and our emotional reactions. My goal is to help them learn how their unconscious and conscious thoughts and feelings affect their relationships and daily lives so they can have more *conscious* control of their thoughts and actions.

Psychoanalysis

Finally, I listen in the fully psychoanalytic mode, with a focus much more on unconscious thoughts and feelings and less on current reality. Current reality is not ever ignored, but it tends to serve as a springboard into the internal world. Psychoanalysis aims to do what we call restructuring the personality: to help the patient to recognize, work through, and resolve the conflicts—the "baggage"—that we all have, so there is less unreasonable guilt and shame, or anger and anxiety can be managed more comfortably, or grief is not overwhelming. The goal is not to achieve happiness, but rather "to face the pain of knowing yourself fully, even when you don't like what you know" (Alperovitz, pers. comm.). To achieve this goal, psychoanalysis focuses on the transference, the feelings that the patient develops about the analyst, as a source of information. Every relationship we have reflects our internal view of the world and of what we expect from relationships; and by observing how the relationship between analyst and patient develops, we can learn a great deal about the patient's internal view of the world.

The distinction between psychoanalysis and psychoanalytic psychotherapy is very fuzzy, and in my practice there is not much difference. In psychotherapy I am somewhat more likely to give occasional advice; in psychoanalysis I am much more likely simply to be silent (and see Mr. Ignatz, on Tuesday, to understand why silence works) or to say, "What do you think?" when asked a question. My analytic patients come more often, three to five times a week, and are encouraged to use the couch so that they are not distracted or influenced by my expression or nonverbal reactions. Lying on the couch encourages us to turn *inward,* to consider our own feelings and thoughts: "The attempt to find words for your internal experience forces you to think more clearly and to move away from the internal chaos. We contain the chaos with words and find ways to speak the unspeakable. As soon as we have done this, it is no longer unspeakable, but can be managed and thought about" (Forester, pers. comm.).

Whether I am engaged in medication monitoring, supportive therapy (less frequent sessions, with a general goal of helping the patients manage their lives without looking too deeply into their feelings), weekly psychotherapy, or formal psychoanalysis, I listen with the psychoanalytic understanding that every communication has both a surface meaning and a deeper meaning that is not consciously spoken. For instance, a patient may report an excellent response to a medication intended to help him to curtail panic attacks, but then miss a follow-up appointment and stop taking the medication. If and when he eventually comes back, again with the symptoms that originally brought him to treatment, I will talk with him about why he stopped the medication. I will consider the possibility that the medication was not helpful enough, or that there were unexpected side effects. I will also consider the possibility that the patient doesn't like taking pills because it makes him feel weak or inadequate ("using a crutch") or crazy (and if you don't take pills you don't have to admit that you're crazy), or because in his family if you are not "crazy" in some way you don't fit (and so you don't want to give up your symptoms), or for some other reason that has not occurred to me. Always, in every situation, I think about conscious external reality—the things we know about and can talk about and that others can recognize in us—as well as internal reality—the things we feel and experience that we are not immediately aware of. That is the analytic approach: the belief that behaviors and conscious thoughts have psychological meaning beyond what we know, and that understanding the meaning is transformative.

About this Book

When I thought about how best to explain how powerful knowing and being known can be, I recognized that discussion of our "internal worlds"—the unconscious thoughts, feelings, and expectations we all have that shape our conscious behavior—is confusing and complicated even when you are familiar with the ideas. I finally decided that I should let you learn about it in the same way I learned it, so I have described a week in my professional life. The patients are, of course, either disguised or fictional, but the quotes are true, and the descriptions of the work are taken entirely from my professional experiences. As I talk about the patients in a typical week, you will read about some of my thoughts, how theory informs what I do, and how sometimes I set theory aside because doing something different seems more effective. You won't learn how to do psychotherapy, but you will see how my professional philosophy and understanding shape my professional behavior, and what the fundamental principles are in my work. You will see when and why I step outside the traditional practices of the work, and how I think about the conflicts among various competing needs to guide the work.

You also will have a chance to see how writing this book has changed me, for some of the same reasons that doing psychotherapy changes the therapist. When I had written about half of the book, I was acutely aware of how my own attitude about the work was being influenced. As a way of being clear for myself about those changes, I wrote some pieces about what I was seeing in myself. It seemed useful to include that reflection to show how being a therapist can change how you see yourself.

About Me

My usual writing style is somewhat distant and does not reveal much about my own thoughts and feelings. Initially, I tried to continue that in this book. I did not want to write a memoir, and am much more comfortable with a certain distance between my readers and me. I suspect that my analytic style—trying not to intrude my own thoughts and issues on my patients—"slops over" to all my thinking about the work, and so into the writing about the work. I realized, however, that (just like in therapy) I could not withhold myself if I wanted to do a good job; and so I resigned myself to writing the memoir that I had never wanted to write. My hope is that reading about how I think about the work will demonstrate the value of this approach.

Because I am an analyst, the transference is the first thing that always comes to my mind. So as I thought about the book, I wondered about how my current patients would react to the book. There are of course many patients described here, and if any of them recognize themselves in the book (which is unlikely, since most of them are not in fact in it), they would be likely to have lots of different feelings. I have of course heavily disguised any patients discussed.

As I thought about how my patients might respond, I imagined how I might feel in a similar place. Even if I had given my own therapist permission to write and publish about me, I might regret it on seeing it in print. I might be angry at having to "share" my analyst with all the readers of the book. Or perhaps I would feel flattered, as if being in the book made me special, a "favored child" to my analyst. If I did not see myself in the book, I might be jealous about being left out. I don't pretend to know all the different ways in which my patients might react, but I certainly know they will react.

I know my patients will react because our patients react to everything we do, sometimes in trivial ways, sometimes in ways that interfere with the treatment. The task of the analyst is to be alert to such reactions, to bring them up for discussion, and to understand what those reactions tell her about the patient. If I find myself not doing something because it might bother my patients, I need to think about why it is so important to me that they not be upset: my job is not to keep my patients calm or happy, but to help them tolerate and understand their reactions—even when the reaction is anger at me—as a way of helping them understand themselves more fully.

Thinking about how my patients would respond to reading about fictional or disguised patients, I also wondered about how they would respond to what this book reveals about me and my internal world. When my first book, *Language and Connection in Psychotherapy: Words Matter* (Davis 2012), was published, many of my patients bought copies of it. Some asked me to sign it for them; some did not tell me they had bought it until months after they had read it, when they remarked on something I had said. I expect to see a similar phenomenon with this book; and in fact it will likely be even more marked as my current patients read the book to understand how I think about them, wondering if the clinical stories I use are about their lives or treatments, no matter how disguised. I expect to find traces of this in transference reactions for years to come, with some patients wondering about whether they might be in a future book. Since I can't know in advance what the reactions will be, or how it will affect future therapy, I will have to wait and let my patients show me what to do in each individual case.

As I thought about how my patients would react to the book, I began to think about my own reaction to it. I have throughout the book written frequently about how therapy grows out of the interaction between therapist and patient; and so the book, which reveals my thoughts and life and work, has to affect and be affected by my interactions with my patients and by my life.

As I wrote, I noticed for the first time how much psychoanalyst Donald Winnicott's work has shaped my own work and my own thoughts about psychotherapy. I read more Winnicott in order to be able to talk about him clearly, and my views of some patients changed in light of what I was reading. As I saw those patients differently, it shifted how I understood what Winnicott was saying about the process. The interaction of my reading, my writing, my patients, and myself was quite striking, with information and understanding flowing back and forth among the four elements repeatedly. You can see some of the results of that process as you read through from Monday to Saturday, with more, and more complex, references to Winnicott in the later days.

Reverie

I also noticed consciously what I already knew unconsciously: that my experience in falling into a reverie in therapy has pervaded my life. My internal reverie (the continual musing about what I am hearing and what it means, discussed in Tuesday's chapter) continues outside the consulting room, and I am more or less attentive to it depending on how much I need to attend to external reality.

On the day I wrote the paragraphs you are reading now, for instance, as I drove to the office I heard part of a National Public Radio program on the effect of music on biological functions such as pain control, and the interaction with the psychological effects of music. My thoughts went to a longtime patient who is a professional musician, and her attempts to communicate emotion to me with music since she could not find words for it. Because music does not have the emotional resonance for me that it does for her, the communication was incomplete and unsatisfactory; and I began to be more aware of how much we can lose emotionally when we try to pin things down with words or in any other way. The effort to be clear, specific, and honest in words inevitably loses some force in translation.

As I thought about that loss of meaning in using words, I was starkly reminded of my struggle in writing this book, where I am trying to talk about things for which there are often no good words. One of the reasons I admire Winnicott is because he seems to be able to evoke emotional awareness in his writing without describing the emotion:

when I read his work, I feel like I know exactly what he means, but I cannot put it into words so I can explain it to someone else.

By the time I got to my office that day, I was aware that this train of thought had some valuable ideas that I wanted to hold onto but that I had to write them down immediately or I'd lose them. If I even spoke briefly to anyone, the thought would be lost. And even as I wrote it down, I knew that it seemed fragmented, unclear, and not as useful as the original associative stream.

Most of the time I don't hold onto these thoughts long enough to write them down, although I think them again later. Once I began working on the book, I started carrying a notebook everywhere so I could capture some of those fleeting thoughts. On the weekend, then, I would go through the notebook to decide where in the book I could include the thoughts I had saved. This in turn brought the reverie outside of the office closer to the surface in my daily life, and made some of those thoughts more accessible to the reverie inside the therapeutic hours.

Everything I experience in my life becomes a part of the ongoing reverie; as we say about our patients' associations, "It's all grist for the mill." Going through my day, whether with a patient or doing something else, I have in the back of my mind a stream of thoughts and associations drawn from all of my experiences, both work and outside-of-work. My personal life is enriched by my work experiences, and my work is enriched by my life experiences.

Writing this book brought home to me that, in a very real way, I cannot keep myself "neutral"; I cannot keep any part of myself out of the consulting room. I am the tool of the work, and that tool is dulled or sharpened by how I live the rest of my life.

Recognizing that I cannot keep any part of myself out of the consulting room and still do good work, I finally recognized that I also could not keep myself out of the book and have it be an honest book.

One of my colleagues who read an early draft remarked that she did not recognize me in the description of my work: "That's not how I know you," she said, referring to the uniformly calm and even tone of my clinical vignettes. So the next revision included more of the emotional drama that I find in the work—not only for my patient, but for myself.

Theory in the Therapy Hour

Thinking about this, I came back to the uses of theory, and how my understanding of theory interacts with my actual experience with the patient. In the room with the patient, I have to be what Heinz Kohut called "experience-near": feeling the affect, resonating in my own internal world with what is communicated both consciously and unconsciously from the patient's internal world. We call our emotional responses to the patient's communication *countertransference*—a counterpart to the transference, the patient's emotional response to the analyst—and today's analysts know that recognizing our countertransference is a vital element of our work. If I cannot do that, I cannot truly listen honestly, hear fully what I am being told, and understand what I am being told.

Once I "get it," I can put the emotional experience and understanding into words, as much as words can convey it (which is never quite enough), and make an interpretation: I can put some part of the patient's internal world into words that he or she can use to understand herself or himself. In that interpretive mode, I step back from the "experience-near" emotional understanding and access the part of my professional self that knows the theory and is one step removed from the emotion. That allows me to contain the emotion for the patient: to remain calm, perhaps even dispassionate.

An example can help to make this process more clear. Some years ago I was seeing a young woman who was unable to give me a clear history about the symptoms that had brought her to me, or indeed about anything in her life. Every time she began to describe a sequence of events she would get distracted and disorganized, and end up telling me about something completely unconnected. As I listened, I became more and more confused and disorganized myself, until I just wanted to say, "Stop! Let's take one thing at a time!"

Instead of interrupting her, I made myself take a step back in my mind and think about what I know about such disorganized thinking. It was not a disorder of cognitive thinking, as I would have seen if the patient was psychotic. Instead, it was an inability to create a narrative about her life that made sense to either of us. Thinking about the disorganization in those terms, I was reminded of research about insecure attachments in people who had abusive or unavailable parents, and the finding that people with insecure attachments are unable to form a coherent narrative about their lives.

With this recognition, I could attune myself to clues about this young woman's attachment patterns—the relationships in her life that were important, and how she managed within those relationships—and find some understanding that allowed me to make sense of what she was telling me. As I looked for those attachment patterns, I recognized her pattern of leaving relationships for no particular reason that she recognized. Since the repeated loss of relationships was distressing to her and was the source of some of her depression, when I commented on that she felt that I understood and might be able to help her make sense of her life. That recognition of a pattern that we could talk about helped *me* to feel less disorganized and confused, and helped *her* to feel understood and at least a little hopeful.

Experience-Near Writing

I have discovered that as I write, I am almost invariably in the interpretive mode, *not* experience-near, and so the entirety of who I am is not in that writing. The interpretive mode can be useful in the therapy hour, when the patient knows me as a real, engaged person and not only the somewhat dispassionate commentator. But my readers do not know me in that way, and so the interpretive mode, and my early drafts of the book, felt as if I was always the dispassionate observer, not ever the real, interpersonally engaged psychotherapist.

My struggle in completing this book has been the same struggle we all have in doing psychotherapy: to be at the same time engaged, alive, and real and simultaneously thoughtful, reflective, and nonintrusive in our relationship with the patient. It sounds like an impossible task, and it is. Perhaps this is why Freud called psychoanalysis an impossible profession. But even when we fail, that failure becomes a part of the work as we talk with our patients about how *they* felt about the failure.

I hope that I succeeded in my attempt to be engaged, alive, and real and simultaneously thoughtful in this description of a week in my professional life. Throughout, I have separated my descriptions of events from my thoughts about events. As I listen to my patients, I need to stay clear about the difference between what my patient has actually said, and what I think about what she or he has said. As a way to help my readers stay clear about that difference, paragraphs that reflect my thoughts about the patient and about the work are indented. The paragraphs that are not indented are about the events of the hour or about external reality.

Chapter 1

My Office, My Practice

As I walk into my office on Monday morning, on the first day back from a family vacation, I am struck with a feeling of "rightness." I have been in practice for more than thirty years, in offices of varying sizes. In training I had one tiny room that I shared with others; after I finished my training, I joined the faculty of a medical college in a large city and had offices provided by the hospital where I taught and directed inpatient services. From that setting, where I had very little space but lots of support from colleagues for my work, I moved after nine years to a private practice where I had more space and colleagues in the area, but no one during the day to discuss the work with.

In 1992 I took a position as medical director at a psychiatric residential treatment center for children and adolescents who were in need of treatment more intensive than could be provided in community settings, but not as intensive as hospitalization. In that setting, again

I had lots of space as well as people to talk to about my work, but because I was the "boss" I seldom felt able to share my uncertainties or struggles. Because of the demands of the job, I also was not able to practice psychoanalytic psychotherapy or psychoanalysis, for which I had spent years in training, and I missed it. In 1995 I came to the community I am in now: a medium-sized city that is in transition from being mostly rural to being a small metropolitan area. Halfway between two large cities, it nevertheless has a small-town feel because of its roots in farming.

In this small-town setting, with few psychiatrists trained to see children, I have become a sort of general practitioner of psychiatry. Like the old-fashioned general practitioner, I see a little bit of everything and do whatever is needed at the time. I have not restricted myself to working only with children, or to psychoanalytic psychotherapy, although that is what I enjoy most in my work, and it is at the foundation of how I think about my work. That sort of therapy—listening as one person tells his or her story, sharing his or her problems and emotional struggles for forty-five minutes once or twice a week over months to years—can be very powerful, and is what I see as a gold standard of treatment.

But not everybody wants that sort of treatment, or needs it, or can use it. Many come seeking medication alone, not realizing that medication alone is not usually adequate for lasting symptom relief. Some are eager or willing for psychotherapy, but cannot tolerate the intensity of the feelings stirred up in more intensive therapy, and so must begin with less frequent sessions and more indirect discussion of issues. Some are not psychologically minded enough, or self-reflective enough, to work in a treatment approach that teaches you to recognize how your own thoughts and feelings affect you. Some live in families where the interactions with other family members are problematic and keep them from finding solutions to their troubles, so that they need family interventions more than individual therapy.

Practice Pattern

My practice model is somewhat idiosyncratic. Most psychiatrists today do very little psychotherapy, seeing many patients for medication only and delegating the psychotherapeutic portion of the treatment (if any) to other professionals. As far as I know, I am the only psychiatrist in my area who does any significant amount of therapy. Because psychiatrists in this area are in short supply, I do a fair amount of medication management but even more psychotherapy. I believe strongly that medication alone is not enough to relieve the psychological suffering of most of my patients, and I need to be able to collaborate closely with the therapist if I am not myself providing the psychotherapy. My policy is that I will usually not see anyone for medication management unless he or she is in psychotherapy with me or with one of the therapists in my office. I work with Janet and Heidi, two experienced therapists (though not themselves analysts) with masters' degrees, one in clinical social work and one in psychology, who are my employees but work independently. All the patients in the office at least start with talking about their problems with one of the three of us. For those who come to this office, we all try to determine what approach will be most helpful, what interventions they are most likely to be able to use effectively, and whether we can provide the help they need.

I consider myself to be a little bit of an outlier, not fitting cleanly into the clinic model, where I would see patients for ten- to twenty-minute medication checks, but also not fitting cleanly into the model of therapist/analyst, whose patients mostly come for forty-five to sixty minutes weekly or more often. I have been lucky enough to be able to work in a way that lets me balance the very real need for my specific medical training—diagnosis and medication management—with the equally real need for a physician who can see both the biochemical aspects of psychiatric illnesses and the psychological needs of the people who suffer from those illnesses. The outlier role is comfortable because for much of my life I have been a little rebellious, finding ways to function outside what traditional authorities expect but to still be the "good girl" who finds approval from those authorities. It would be true to say that my nontraditional practice model is not only clinically useful, but that it satisfies a psychological need for me.

The "rightness" I feel today is because now I am working with two therapists who I know and trust, and who know and trust me; and we share our thoughts and puzzles about the work so that none of us feel isolated. I also have been able to establish my own physical space, which meets my own needs and is decorated to suit those needs, and I have established a psychological space that meets my needs as well.

Waiting Room

Entering the office, I walk into a large waiting room decorated in soft colors, with pictures on the wall that reflect my own tastes. In a nook in one corner is a colorful and cartoonish "Jonah and the Whale" hanging over a child-sized table, with child-sized chairs and children's books.

In the larger area of the waiting room are ten armchairs and a table with magazines. The walls hold abstract versions of landscapes, colorful but not loud. The wallpaper is in soft grays and pale blues, and the pictures are mostly peaceful, in pastels with some splashes of color. The chairs are left from the previous tenant, an orthodontist, and are a somewhat grim brown, but they are comfortable. A multi-CD player usually plays soft music of varying types ranging from classical to soft rock.

My office staff and I have tried to create the feeling of a comfortable living room. Most of my patients do find the waiting room comforting and peaceful; one or two will deliberately come early for their appointments to be able to sit in the peace and quiet.

It has been said that the office setting is the analyst's first clinical intervention, and the tone of the office often sets the tone for the treatment. We have tried to create a "holding environment" (Winnicott 1960) in which people can feel comfortable, safe, and contained as they face the turmoil within. I know from experience that without that sort of "holding" and containment, little other psychological work gets done.

Front Office

At the desk where my secretary Patty works are two right-angled stretches of desktop with phones, a computer, and the schedules for myself and the therapists who work for me. There is an S-shaped hall stretching to the right that leads to the file room and my own consulting room.

Private Office

My consulting room is round, larger than most therapists' offices, and large enough to need "sizing down" with three low bookcases in an arc curving away from the door. The bookcases are in the middle of the room so that the space where I sit with patients is not too roomy to be cozy. There are other low bookcases along the walls of the room. Walking in, I pass a six-foot Norfolk Island pine between bookcases on the right. On the other side of the room is a large wooden dollhouse, usually with furniture and dolls jumbled and in disarray, as well as a counter holding many stuffed animals—Cookie Monster, a wallaby, several cats, a shark, a rabbit, and others. I have collected these stuffed animals one by one over the years for play therapy, and never get rid of any of them. The animals fill two of the three sinks in the counter, which were left from when the orthodontist used this room for his dental hygienists; and a mirror behind the animals reflects the room, making it feel even larger.

The needs of the orthodontist dictated that his hygienists worked in a circle in the middle of the room, so the room is round. For me it offers odd spaces in what would otherwise be corners, and in those spaces I have different things: a large stuffed penguin with his baby penguin; an extra chair for when I see families; a piece of art on a tall, skinny table.

All the bookcases in the room hold a collection of books about psychoanalysis, psychiatry, and psychotherapy, with many journal collections and the collected works of Freud and Anna Freud, and as I come in, occasionally I notice a book I would like to read or re-read. The tops of the bookcases hold various *tchotchkes*, miscellaneous small pieces of memorabilia, most given to me by patients. One of my favorites, in the arc of bookcases at the center of the room, is a curved wooden sculpture that I have always believed was an abstract version of a person holding arms to contain something not seen (I imagine a mother holding her baby). Another favorite, often commented on by patients, is on the middle bookcase: three bronze coyotes pacing in a circle with a metal snake curving around their feet, on a metal base that fills the surface. On the left bookcase is a tall, thin-legged metal elephant. Past the bookcases is the analytic couch, a fainting couch done in blue tapestry, with two comfortable black leather chairs facing it. My dull-green leather reclining chair is at the head of the couch next to an oval table with a top that swings around to allow me access to writing space. By each chair is a small table with a Kleenex box and a trashcan.

The table next to me has several shelves filled with notebooks and paper. On the swinging top of the table are a note pad, my prescription pad, a small ivory Buddha, an ivory netsuke of a dragon, and many pens. On my right, past the table, is a low cabinet with drawers; it holds several family pictures, as well as a large art piece—flowing sand in a frame that turns to allow the sand to make new patterns—hiding most of the pictures. I also have a cardholder with some of my business cards on that cabinet.

My desk, with my laptop computer and various papers, faces the wall next to the dollhouse and is flanked on the left by a cabinet with papers, a printer, and books to be read. To the right is a built-in wall cabinet with a sound system that doesn't work (left by the orthodontist and too expensive to remove) and many cubbyholes of different sizes. Occasionally patients will ask if I use the sound system to record sessions, and I've come to recognize that sort of suspicion as a clue to how that person sees the world.

On the wall the patients face, behind me and over the couch, are four paintings representing the four seasons of an Asian landscape in shades of gray, and an orange-and-red wooden cat done in collapsing slats, with pegs for hanging hats. On the wall to my left—to the patients' right as we sit—are large art pieces with diagrams in green fuzz, which are clearly engines of some sort. On the opposite wall are another piece in green fuzz, several clear boxes with geometric, complicated three-dimensional pieces that look like machines, a black-and-white Rorschach-looking picture, and a geometric and abstract Cat in the Hat. These are all pieces done by my nephew, a professional artist, and are odd enough to stir remarks from people new to the office. I was complimented on the room recently by a patient who sees it as having "lots of things to look at when you need distraction" (which she frequently does), "but everything can mean whatever you need it to mean."

There are also three clocks on the walls: one visible to patients on the couch, one behind me visible to patients in the chairs facing me, and one on the wall opposite me. The third clock was added at the request of a patient who specifically wanted *not* to have to see me look to the side to check the time.

Neutrality and Self-Disclosure in Office Decor

I wonder sometimes if people see me as preoccupied with time, but I know that time is an important part of the frame of therapy. The process of analytic psychotherapy is simultaneously timeless and time-bounded, and both are important. The sessions begin and end at specific times because they must to allow for scheduling and because we must return to everyday life at some point. They are simultaneously timeless because both patient and therapist know that we will be back tomorrow, or next week, and the conversation that is interrupted now can continue then. The clocks remind us of the role of time in the work done in this room.

When we were setting up the office, I wondered about how personal I should make the wall decorations and the office décor in general. Many psychoanalysts try not to reveal much of themselves in their office décor, because we are taught that we need to be neutral, that if we do not show who we are the patient will, in their minds, make us who they need us to be in order to satisfy their unconscious scripts about relationships. If we are a blank slate, unknown to our patients, we can find out a great deal about them by understanding who they imagine us to be; this is what we call transference, and understanding the transference is at the center of the work we do.

Experience has taught us, however, that we cannot ever be truly neutral. We are ourselves the tools of the work, and our exploration of the patient's inner world is filtered through our personalities and through the interaction between our patients and ourselves. In that interaction, we inevitably reveal ourselves to our patients. Our patients notice our "mood, style of dress, voice tone, facial expression, body tension, signs of fatigue or illness, use of silence, and use of talking, and [they begin] to consider how these things might relate to the therapist's values and opinions, surges of energy following vacations, and all other manner of verbal and nonverbal phenomena that contribute to the definition of the therapist as a person" (Maroda 2004, 67). One patient can tell when my absences are because I am attending professional conferences as opposed to simple vacations: she notes that after conferences I am always "sharper" and more direct (and apparently a little scary to her) when I comment about the meaning of her communications.

Patrick Casement (1991, 53) notes that, "Analysts and therapists often give away more about themselves than they realize. They might not speak openly about themselves, and they can be careful about personal questions, but they do not remain a closed book to the patient." He tells us that patients will not see their analysts as blank screens, but will be very alert to what they can find out about us. My patients monitor changes in my state of relaxation or my fidgeting, and the unconscious implications of the nature of my comments (for example, "You seemed to be a little angry about what my sister said," when I think I have no expression and no change in tone as I speak); they notice the selection and timing of my remarks, wondering why I comment on one thing and not on another; they wonder if I am anxious when I am more or less talkative than usual. In Casement's words, "At least unconsciously, and sometimes consciously, patients will be interpreting the therapist to themselves. They even offer unconscious interpretations to the therapist" (p. 53). They always notice how ready or unready I am to stay in touch with what is being communicated, if I notice or ignore clues that something is going on that is being talked around or actively avoided.

Since I cannot hide myself anyway, I have decided that a more natural sharing of who I am, through the items in my office and through a refusal to keep secrets about my life, allows a freer exchange with the patient, and ultimately I learn more about the patient. Being willing to have items in my office that reflect my tastes and my interests also helps me to relax. It creates a "holding environment" for me as well as for my patients. When I am more comfortable, it is easier to stay grounded in my understanding of myself and remember that my emotional responses to my patients can be understood both as elicited by the patient's behavior and as arising from my own internal conflicts and issues. That, in turn, helps me tolerate the strong emotions that sometimes come up while I listen.

My willingness to be known does not mean that I automatically answer any questions I am asked about myself. The psychotherapeutic relationship is often very intense, and it is very common for patients to want to become a part of our private lives, to want social relationships with us, and to be curious about our inner worlds. If we allow this, however, the focus of the treatment moves away from the patient, which risks making the therapeutic relationship more about us than about our patients.

Although I show who I am in my office, in my behavior, and in how I dress, and I don't hesitate to let my patients know some things about my personal life, I also try to think about what that knowledge might mean to each patient before I answer questions. I often will be heard saying, for instance, "Before I answer that question about myself, we need to think about what it would mean to you to not know; or to know something that you don't expect or don't like." If I do answer questions, such as where I went on vacation, if I am visiting family, if I have children or grandchildren, I try always to ask later what it felt like for the patient to know that: both that I was willing to tell them, and that they now know some of the details of my life. As I write, it occurs to me that even the placement of my family pictures conveys this attitude: I don't mind that people can see my family, but they have to make a visible effort (because of the sand art that blocks them) and that gives us a chance to talk about what they imagine about what they see.

One of the fundamental principles of the way I work is remembering that it requires two people to succeed. What we call the *therapist-patient dyad* is the center of everything that happens in this room, and part of my task is to monitor that dyad and to remember both halves of it as together we try to understand what my patient brings to the room.

Chapter 2

Monday

This week, Monday is my first day back from a week-long vacation, and there are several charts out for me to review. There usually are at least one or two, and after I take off my coat and put away my purse I look at the charts with their accompanying messages and requests for prescription refills. I check the charts for dose and timeliness (meaning, is it a request for an early refill? How long since I last saw the patient?), and then give them back to Patty, my secretary, who will call the prescriptions to the pharmacy once I okay them. I take the messages down the hall to my consulting room with me, thinking about what my day will include.

In my consulting room, I sit at the desk, look at my schedule, and go to the file room next door to pull charts for that day. Sometimes I think about what is likely to come up with that day's patients; usually, though, I just wait to find out what the patients bring, instead of trying to anticipate.

I have learned I usually can't anticipate. Often I remember Wilfred Bion's instruction (1967) to approach our patients "without memory or desire": that is, don't assume that what the patient talked about yesterday will come up today, and don't be wedded to a particular outcome, but let the patient determine what happens. I think of my task as being to provide an emotional space in which my patients can find out about themselves. I need to provide a *neutral* space, one that allows the patient to explore and find himself or herself as much as possible without "impingement" by my own thoughts, feelings, or expectations. (Winnicott 1960).

Free Associations

My patients come to each session with memories of their lives, memories of the relationship with me, memories of why they came to see me, and all the feelings that accompany those memories. They also come with thoughts about the memories and with the feelings that go with those thoughts. For instance, a woman who has just had a fight with her husband may be thinking about a first failed marriage, about other relationships that went wrong, about what her husband did to make her mad, about other people who have disappointed her or made her angry. All of these connected thoughts, which we call associations, are in the mix of information available to the patient; and I ask my patients to say, as best they can, whatever goes through their minds, and to try not to censor the thoughts.

Most of us cannot let ourselves associate freely in this way; we stop ourselves from uncomfortable trains of thought. Often we don't want to share our associations with others because of embarrassment or because we want to preserve our privacy. In therapy, we aim to free up the patient's ability to associate more freely, and we encourage our patients to share their free associations with us.

As I sit with each patient, I have my own memories of recent weeks, my own memories of my life, of my training and experience. With the beginning of the session, as I let myself move from my own internal world into what I know about my patient's internal world, my memories of experiences with each patient begin to take priority over other thoughts and memories. These memories also come with thoughts and accompanying feelings: I may remember another patient who had a similar relationship problem, or remember previous events and discussions with this patient. I may remember something in the patient's life, or from our previous therapy sessions, that initially seems unconnected, and then I wonder about what in the current material brought that thought to mind. If I can identify what brought it to mind and the connection seems helpful, I will tell the patient about the association, and together we will think about what new thoughts and feelings come up then in both the patient and in myself.

For each of us, there are two realities: the external reality, which includes events and facts that people around us would also recognize, and the internal reality, which includes our own perceptions of the world, our expectations about others and about ourselves, and our own individual ways of understanding the outside world. Internal reality is shaped by past experience and by a tendency to see the present in terms of the past—to expect that what has happened before is likely to happen again. For instance, a person who was abused as a child may expect all authority figures to be controlling and mean or openly abusive. The unconscious part of ourselves responds to the external reality, but it is much more dominated by the internal reality. And a therapist must find ways of recognizing and responding to both internal and external realities for both the patient and for herself.

Unconscious Communications

None of us can know our unconscious wishes, fears, or thoughts without help. We suppress (consciously and deliberately refuse to think about something) or repress (are unable to think about or simply choose not to remember) the thoughts, feelings, and events that are most painful or frightening for us ... but clues to the unconscious conflicts appear in derivative forms that others can recognize. An excellent example of this is the "Freudian slip" (named such because Freud was the first to describe it, in *The Psychopathology of Everyday Life)*, such as saying, "I hate it when my father is so demanding," when we mean to complain about our boss. Almost everyone recognizes such slips as signals about feelings that we don't intend to talk about. Calling your girlfriend by your ex-girlfriend's name is a Freudian slip, and usually both you and your girlfriend know that it means you are thinking about the ex.

What a therapist does is recognize the unconscious communications and put them into words in ways that the patient can understand and accept. When we do that, the patient can consciously think about the ideas that had been repressed because they were too painful or frightening. When those ideas can be thought about consciously, the patient's current, adult self can deal with them. Until they can be consciously thought about, the only way the person has to manage the feelings that go with the thoughts is to deny and repress.

As I try to start each session without memory or desire, I try to stay open to both unconscious and conscious communication: both what the patient tells me verbally and what the patient hints at in his behavior or in the way she tells me things. I try to wait to know what is being hinted at unconsciously instead of assuming I know before the patient can tell me. I try not to push the patient toward what I am thinking, but to let the patient decide where to go. New therapists will often ask things such as, "Can I tell the patient he married someone just like his mother?" No, you can't, because it may not be true: you can listen as he describes his interactions with his wife, you can comment on similar patterns that you recognize, but you don't really know how his wife is like or unlike his mother until he himself tells you.

Transference

As a part of being open to the unconscious communication from the patient, I try to be open to recognizing the transference: how the patient feels about me, and how the patient sees me. This will sometimes be remarkably accurate, and some of my patients know things about my personality or my life that I have never told them. Sometimes they know things about me that I don't yet know about myself.

Sometimes their perceptions of me will be off the mark, because in their own internal world they are not yet ready to recognize how their past history distorts their understanding of the behaviors of others. It's very common, for instance, for patients to believe that I disapprove of what they have done, when in fact all I did was to ask about their reason for doing it (and may in fact think it was a positive step for them). People who are very self-critical, or who have been criticized a lot by parents and other authorities, will tend to expect criticism from me, and so they see my question as implied criticism. One of the ways I recognize such unconscious reactions is to pay particular attention to events in the relationship between the patient and me, trying to pick up on how they are reacting to those events.

Today, because I am returning from an absence, I will try throughout the day to notice the reactions of my patients to that absence. Some will have been glad of the break; some will feel as if I abandoned them; for some it will have made no difference at all.

Once I have organized myself for the day as best I can, usually I go back out to the front desk and sit there with a cup of coffee, playing solitaire on the computer and chatting with Patty while I wait for my 8:00 a.m. patient. Unless I overslept, I usually have ten to fifteen minutes of peace, and I have found that if I have this quiet "space" before I begin my clinical day, I am more able to be the "blank slate" that can meet the patient without memory or desire.

First Appointment of the Day

Most often I start my week with Ms. Austin, who is in a formal psychoanalysis and so comes four times a week, always at 8:00 a.m. A middle-aged woman in a demanding profession, she has struggled with depression for most of her life. In our several years of work together, it has been clear that she has a strong need to be liked by other people, and she tends to put others first in all her relationships. For the most part, this is not a problem for her; but not infrequently she puts others first at her own expense. Today, she has cancelled her appointment with me because she has a professional speaking engagement in another city.

Missed Sessions

Many analysts and therapists charge for missed sessions or for late (less than twenty-four hours) cancellations. Some analysts, especially older or more traditional analysts, charge for *any* cancellation. In my own analysis, my analyst charged me for all missed sessions, once even when I was absent because of a major snowstorm in which I could not get out of my apartment parking lot. The principle is that we make our living by selling our time, and when we have reserved a time for a patient and then they do not use that time, it is a financial loss for us (Langs, pp.120–138).

Cancellations often also become a clinical issue, because our patients use this behavior, as they potentially do almost any behavior, to communicate with us. I learned this lesson very early on, when a man I was seeing cancelled at the last minute, ostensibly because he had an unexpected court hearing required by his work. We had been talking about his tendency to be somewhat irresponsible at work, so I felt it was appropriate *not* to charge for the appointment as a way to encourage his responsible behavior (forgetting that the task of the analyst/therapist is not to manipulate behavior change, but to understand what drives the behavior). In his next session, this individual told me somewhat sheepishly that he could in fact have kept his appointment, because his partner could have gone to the court hearing and it would not have made any difference at all. He had, however, not wanted to continue the discussion we had been having in the previous session, so he postponed it for a week by cancelling.

These days I usually do not charge for cancelled sessions, even late cancellations, probably because of my own unresolved issues about taking money for something I haven't done. In my professional adult self, I recognize this as a small deviation from what I was taught, but I have still chosen not to charge except in situations where it becomes clear the patient is abusing my laxity in a way that interferes with the treatment.

Sometimes I see that a particular patient is cancelling or missing sessions as a way of avoiding something in the treatment, and when I try to address it with them they dodge the issue. In those cases, as a way of forcing the issue, I will let them know that I will begin to charge for any more late cancellations or missed sessions. Usually it requires only the notice that I will begin charging, or one charge for a missed session, and then the patient begins to talk about what he or she has been avoiding.

Today, I am sorry not to see Ms. Austin because she is pleasant and works easily and well, and sessions with her are almost always interesting; but I am simultaneously glad to have the time to deal with some of the messages, forms to fill out, and mail that accrued during my vacation. I get a cup of coffee and sit at my desk throwing away junk mail and filling out forms until my 9:00 a.m. patient arrives.

A New Patient

This relatively young man is new to me. He has been seen several times by Janet, one of the therapists in the office, and now comes for a discussion about possible medication. As usual, Janet responded to the initial intake call, making sure he understands that I will not see him for medication unless he is in psychotherapy with Janet, Heidi, or me. People who want only medication will be referred elsewhere. In that initial call, Janet also found out a little about what sort of help this young man was looking for.

This arrangement allows us to be sure that our office is appropriate for the caller. We can make an initial judgment about whether we can provide what will be needed, and if not we will refer the patient elsewhere. For instance, individuals with substance abuse issues generally require a much more directive approach than I use, with lots of limit-setting and focus on environmental issues; individuals with active psychotic disorders most likely should be hospitalized until they are more stable. If the individual is being coerced into therapy by a spouse or a parent, we can also start to disengage the patient from the coercion, ensuring that they are themselves interested in the therapeutic process. If an individual will require a lot of ancillary services (social services, especially, such as help with money management), we will refer elsewhere, since we do not have those resources. On a purely practical level, this screening also allows me to avoid seeing people who are really only interested in medication, since they will likely drop out of treatment before they get to see me. Occasionally an individual will call specifically looking for psychoanalysis, or who has been referred personally to me by another physician, an analyst in another city, or a colleague, and I will generally see those people without screening.

In my first contact with a patient, I greet them in the waiting room as "Mr. or Ms. X" or (if a child) by their first name only, for confidentiality and out of respect, and invite them back to my office. In the office, with a child or adolescent my first remark is a question about whether they understand why they are there; and I will say, "What I tell the very little kids is that I'm a doctor, but not the sort of doctor that gives shots or looks in your eyes or ears. I listen to kids and talk with kids who are unhappy or who are having problems growing up; and your mom" (or dad or grandmom) "wanted me to talk with you and find out how I might be able to help." I am careful to clarify, both for parent and child, that I think not only about medication but also about if things need to change at home or at school, or about anything else I can think of that might help. I then let them know that I will be speaking with the child and whatever adult accompanies them together first, and then will send the adult out of the room so the child can talk with me alone. With very young children, I invite them to play with the toys in the room while I talk with mother or father (if the child wants) and let them know that if they want to say something while I am talking with mother or father they are welcome to do so, or they can wait until it's just us.

With adults, as with this young man, I begin by asking, "How can I help you?"

"I'm not sure."

"Of course—that's why you're here! I should have said, 'What are you looking for help with?'"

He tells me why he has come to see me, and I listen for details of his "presenting complaint," what symptoms are troubling him, and what ideas he has had about what is causing his symptoms. I pay attention as he talks to how he tells me as well as what he tells me.

Some people are unable to provide a coherent story about why they have come to see me, but provide various disjointed reports of symptoms or events that have disturbed them; these individuals, we know now, most likely have an "insecure attachment" (Ainsworth et al), which has implications for their ability to have healthy and stable relationships with others. In my first book, *Language and Communication in Psychotherapy: Words Matter* (Davis 2012), I discuss some of the ways in which how patients tell us their stories also tells us about them as individuals. I describe a young man who lived his life, and who spoke with me, with no observable coherence; he spoke "rapidly, with abrupt shifts of idiom, sentence, and topic," (p. 32) and I often felt that I was missing the point of what he was saying. I also describe a young woman who talked rapidly and nonstop, in a disjointed, tangential manner that was difficult to follow, and who was clearly very anxious. I remark that, "for each of these patients, the form of their linguistic expression shaped what they communicated, and what I was able to understand, about their internal world. This in turn shaped my sense of relatedness to them, below the level of my conscious awareness. In no case was the shaping of the communication conscious: rather it was itself shaped by, and was a reflection of, their internal world" (p. 33).

So when I ask Mr. Barnes about what he is looking for help with, and listen without interrupting to how he describes his problems, I am able to find out not only about his specific symptoms, but about his relationships with others and about how he functions in the world as a whole. Each interview is different, driven by what the patient tells me and what he or she seems to need at the time. In general, by the end of the initial interview I aim to have some sense of when the symptoms began, whether there have been similar symptomatic episodes in the past, whether there has been previous treatment and if so what was helpful, and how much the symptoms interfere with the patient's daily functioning. I also want specifically to know if there is an immediate element of suicidal thinking, and what the risk might be of suicidal actions; if there are panic attacks (an acute fear that something life-threatening is about to happen, with shortness of breath, palpitations, and other physical symptoms of acute anxiety); and if any problems with thinking and concentration interfere with the patient's ability to work or to care for children in the household. These latter three symptoms are things that usually spur me to recommend medication: I believe that the first priority is to make it possible for the patient's daily life to proceed as close to "normal" as we can achieve, so as to minimize the damage done by the symptoms. In ongoing treatment, then, we can take our time in understanding the problems, without having to worry about the fall-out from job loss or disrupted relationships or suicide attempts.

Some patients will ask if I have heard their history from Janet or Heidi, and may not want to have to tell the story a second time. My personal preference is that I not have a lot of history before seeing the patient, both because I tend not to remember it unless I hear it myself, and because I prefer to form my own impressions before learning what someone else thought. I have learned over the years that when my own initial impression is significantly different from that of Heidi or Janet, it helps to explore why we have those different impressions, and what the difference can tell us about the patient. Because we each have our own different histories, we react unconsciously to different parts of the patient's story, and comparing those reactions can help us to understand how he has emphasized various parts differently with different people.

By the end of the interview with Mr. Barnes, I have created a tentative *diagnostic formulation*, a story that explains his symptoms to a greater or lesser degree (for example, anxiety, depression, post-traumatic stress disorder, a psychotic disorder). I have some ideas about what the psychological origins of his symptoms are most likely to be, including some hints about early life experiences and how they shaped his way of being in the world; what relief medication may or may not bring; how self-reflective he is and how much he is likely to be able to use psychotherapy along with medication; and what general approach is most likely to be useful in the psychotherapy. It is clear in today's interview that Mr. Barnes has considerable performance anxiety, which keeps him from concentrating and focusing at work. It also gets in the way with his wife and children, because his work anxiety keeps him from being able to be relaxed and available for them at home.

Mr. Barnes has apparently always been somewhat perfectionistic, and it is important to him to be seen as competent and capable. About eighteen months ago, his employer lost some contracts; and although the work problems were not due to Mr. Barnes's performance, he blamed himself and reacted with self-criticism and an increase in what he expected from himself. He is now working extra hours in an attempt to be "better," but is unable to think clearly and be productive; and at home he is irritable and withdrawn. He has started having trouble sleeping, and shows most of the signs of a clinical depression.

I tell Mr. Barnes what I think is causing his symptoms, naming it specifically as depression with associated anxiety, and recommend a medication that is helpful for both depression and anxiety. I describe the potential side effects of the medication, what he can expect in results (including that most psychiatric medications take several weeks to take effect), and what we might do if the initial medication is ineffective or does not control all his symptoms. I remind him that the reason I will not prescribe medication unless he is in therapy at the same time is because medication brings quicker relief but psychotherapy offers lasting change. We talk briefly about his experience with Janet, and how the psychotherapy can help him to understand the beginnings of his depression and anxiety. He agrees to my recommendation for medication along with psychotherapy, and we make a second, brief appointment to evaluate how effective the medication is. I let him know that although I try to return phone calls, I am not always as good at it as I might wish, and that if his call is urgent, he should say so and I will call back before I go home that day. And I tell him that he will get better treatment if he is "a little pushy," and doesn't hesitate to tell me if he thinks that I am not listening, or that I have not understood what he is saying. We then say good-bye, and he leaves, stopping at the front desk to pay his bill. I will, later in the day, discuss Mr. Barnes and my impressions with Janet, comparing notes about what we heard from him and what we each thought about his initial problems. It is my impression that he is most likely to gain significant relief from the medication; but more importantly, that he is self-reflective enough to be able to use the work with Janet to find new ways of dealing with his self-criticism and perfectionism.

Medication Monitoring

After Mr. Barnes, I have three people scheduled for "med checks": appointments focused primarily on the medication they are prescribed and how they are responding. They will all be people I have seen for an initial evaluation, like Mr. Barnes, and so I know them a little. Some of them I have seen every month for some time; some I have seen every three months for a year or longer.

My practice is that when I first see someone about medication, I see them monthly or more often until we are satisfied that we have accomplished what we can with medication; then I see them every three months to make sure the medication continues to work and that they are not developing side effects. When we reach the "every three months" stage, usually I will offer them the option of returning to their primary care physician (internist, family doctor, pediatrician, gynecologist) for routine monitoring. For uncomplicated situations, where the patient is on a single antidepressant or an antidepressant and a medication for anxiety, most of the medications are familiar to the primary care physicians in the area, and they are willing to provide the routine monitoring and take responsibility for writing prescriptions. I do always emphasize to these patients that if problems come up, or if the medication seems to stop working, they are very welcome to return to my office for care. I try to discourage people from returning to see me for routine prescriptions, since it would be very easy for my days to fill up with people who come in for ten minutes to get prescriptions for the same medications they have been taking for two years. Although this would be lucrative, and relatively easy, it also is not particularly interesting to me, and I prefer not to do much routine medication monitoring.

After seeing Mr. Barnes, I have an appointment with Mr. Copperfield, who has been stable on his medications for some years, with occasional disruptions that require a brief shift in his doses; he has bipolar disorder with a complicated medication regimen that requires a specialist to monitor it. In addition, Mr. Copperfield is involved in individual psychotherapy with Janet. He came to us when his previous psychiatrist retired, and he had never had a significant period of individual psychotherapy to help him understand himself and his response to his disease and his medication. Janet, Mr. Copperfield, and I are all clear that his bipolar disorder causes major problems in his marriage and his life, but we are all also clear that he manages those problems more effectively because of the work he has done with Janet. He is more able to recognize warning signs of an increase in mood lability; when he is more depressed, or is becoming manic and irritable, he is more able now to step back and stop his negative interactions with family. He is still, after several years, seeing Janet weekly, and taking the time to understand what sorts of life stresses or emotional dilemmas tend to push him toward becoming more depressed or more irritable and manic. I have found that when I meet with him it is most productive if I take the time not only to review what he thinks about his medication, but to hear what he thinks about stresses in his life that have stirred up emotional discomfort. He is very familiar with his medications and how they affect his mood, and each time we meet he is able to tell me how well or how poorly he feels the medication is controlling his mood swings.

Today Mr. Copperfield is coming out of a period of increased depression and irritability and is back to his usual level of functioning, so the appointment is relatively brief and uncomplicated. As he is leaving my office, he stops and says, "I'm feeling more in control of myself than I ever have. I want to thank you and Janet. I'm a better person because of you."

After about five minutes, my next patient, arrives: Ms. Dockerty is a middle-aged woman who came to me when she and her husband moved to this community. She had a very severe, life-threatening depression that was extraordinarily resistant to treatment, and in another community required some unusually aggressive treatment. By the time she arrived in this area, she was stable and doing well, although she was on very high doses of several medications. Because she was stable, and had been for some years, we agreed to very cautiously try to reduce the doses of her medications. Over several years, we have been able to reduce her medication doses to those that are in the more usual range, and she is now coming in only every three months to make sure that things continue to go well. We talk about events in her life and activities she's enjoying, which lets me get a sense for whether her depression is still in remission or is beginning to emerge again. She is in individual therapy elsewhere (an exception to my usual practice), but when we meet she tells me about the things in her life that are particularly stressful. Like Mr. Copperfield, Ms. Dockerty is fairly self-reflective and is aware of the sorts of issues in her life that pose a risk for stirring up her internal conflicts and starting her back on the road to depression; she has on a few occasions called for an urgent appointment because she was afraid she was slipping back into her depressive state, but each time she has been able to ward it off. Today, our conversation feels like catching up with a friend, and I get to experience the pleasure of success without the labor it usually requires to get there.

Ms. Dockerty's appointment is also relatively short because she is doing well, and so I am able to return a phone call from the weekend before I see Ms. Eakins, a young woman who had a "nervous breakdown" at college, was hospitalized, and came to me for medication management when she took a leave from school and came home. She also is doing well, and we have been reducing the doses of medication that she was placed on in hospital. When I first saw her, she complained of a "brain fog" that kept her from thinking clearly, and it was my hope that reducing her medication doses would clear that up. As we talk today,

I listen closely to her patterns of thought as reflected in her speech to assess whether they have returned to her original level of functioning. I try to engage her in discussing life events, especially the things at school that have seemed most stressful, but she turns most inquiries away with a noncommittal, "Everything's going great!"

Her recovery has not been as complete as I had hoped, but she has now been able to stop the medication that is most likely to have been the cause of the "brain fog" without any return of her original symptoms of anxiety and confusion. She is seeing Heidi for psychotherapy, but seems not particularly interested in understanding herself, and I suspect that the psychotherapy will be a relatively brief experience. I also suspect that she will never engage deeply in treatment, but that once her symptoms are contained she will drop out, quite possibly even stop taking her medication. I regret that, because I believe her "nervous breakdown" was due to life stresses that are likely to recur, and she is at risk for further problems if she doesn't find some way to be more comfortable with them and with herself.

It's not uncommon that a patient leaves treatment without really having accomplished anything except to treat the symptoms without addressing the root cause of those symptoms—much like repeatedly taking Tylenol for a headache without figuring out why the headache keeps coming back—and I always am a little sad to see that. However, I was able many years ago to come to terms with knowing that not everybody wants to know about themselves, and that I can't make people do what is "best" for them. I know that my job is not to "fix" them, but to help them achieve their own goals for their lives, letting go of what I think might be better. I try always to make an effort to engage them in deeper work, but if they resist—like Ms. Eakins—I let it go.

48

When I begin with people like Ms. Eakins or Ms. Dockerty, trying to reduce medication doses without a return of the symptoms that led to the medication in the first place, I am very careful. I seldom make more than one change at a time; I make only a very small change; and I wait at least a month before making other changes. In evaluating the results of psychiatric medications, it is always a question of whether the ups and downs of the patient's mood and functioning are due to the medication changes, or whether they are due to life stresses; so I try to wait out most stressful periods without making changes so as not to upset the patient's functioning. I also will always talk with my patients about what has been going on in their lives for the time since our last appointment, with particular emphasis on stresses and/or times of poor functioning, trying to get a feeling for what sorts of events in their lives might trip off their symptoms.

I try always to remember the dictum to "do no harm," which to me means not doing something that would create chaos in the patient's functioning and life. My insistence on concurrent psychotherapy is useful here, as subtle problems with overall functioning are much more likely to be noticed by the individual therapist (whether me or someone else) than in a brief medication-focused visit.

It's always a pleasure for me to see several people in a row who are doing well, and who can begin coming off their medications. I don't particularly like using medication because so often symptom relief keeps people from going on with psychotherapy (like Ms. Eakins), which I believe is more useful in the long run. I do know sometimes medication is necessary to preserve functioning; and being able to discontinue some medications helps me to persist in the (unfounded) hope that when I eventually retire I will feel less like I am abandoning my patients.

Gifts

Again I have a few minutes to return phone calls before I see my next patient, Ms. Flato. She is a middle-aged woman who has been coming once or twice a week for about a year, for help with feeling "stuck" in her life. She is clearly unhappy, knows what she is unhappy with, but has not been able to motivate herself to take the steps she needs to make changes. In the year we have been working together, at first weekly and now (at her request) twice weekly, she has been able to recognize some significant patterns in her life that have contributed to the "stuckness," and she is beginning to get her financial affairs in order so she can get out of a stagnant and unrewarding relationship. My work with Ms. Flato is generally interesting and satisfying because she shows obvious progress and is very appreciative of feeling better.

I'm not completely clear in my own mind about what has been most helpful to Ms. Flato. There have been no startling insights, simply a slow process of increasing clarity about how she feels and about how she sees her relationships with others, including how she slowly allowed the "stuckness" to creep up on her. I believe that Donald Winnicott's ideas about the "nonprescriptive analyst" are helpful here. He suggests that the "nonprescriptive analyst" creates a space in which the patient can develop in her own way rather than doing what the analyst (or anyone else) wants, and that seems to be what Ms. Flato is achieving for herself

Ms. Flato has a tendency to want to bring me gifts: small bags of candy she likes, an offering of a book she's found that she enjoyed. She does this partly because she appreciates our work together, but also because this is how she relates to people she likes: she enjoys helping others, enjoys giving them pleasure, and she needs to feel that she has something to give the rest of the world.

The issue of gifts can be thorny for therapists who focus on the relationship as part of the work. We are, generally, taught that we should not accept gifts, that it is a boundary violation and inappropriate. My own thoughts about that issue are less black and white. A large gift, one that is expensive or which the patient can't truly afford, is of course inappropriate, and should be refused tactfully. We must, as therapists, keep in mind the priority of understanding what the gift means to the patient, why they felt the wish or need to bring us the gift, and as we refuse the gift we often will raise the question at that point for discussion.

I believe that smaller gifts may be important not to refuse. Our patients want to know that we value the relationship as much as they do, and often they feel that we have given them so much that they want to give back. We know that we have "given" them, really, nothing—we have done the work that we are paid for—but for them, it is something that they do not get anywhere else. Ms. Flato's gifts would fall in this category.

For others, exploring the meaning of the gift can tell us something important about the patient. I remember the woman, years ago, who brought me small gifts at least once a month for some time before I was able to get her to talk about what they meant. When she finally was able to talk about it, she said that the gifts were "in the nature of throwing virgins into the volcano": she was almost terrified that I would be angry with her or would become dangerous in some way, and the gift was to placate me. That fear of my anger, and of the relationship, was at the center of how this woman related to most of the people in her life, and the chance to talk about it with her was a continuing thread in her treatment for many years.

For children especially, gifts in both directions can be important: a way to show the child that you value the relationship, and to allow the child to show you that he or she values it equally. Children will often ask to take home some of the toys in the office, perhaps as a way to "take home" the memory of the relationship with you. In that situation, I will usually not allow them to take the toy, as I need it for the other children I see (and in fact, sometimes the child wants to take it to keep it away from the other children that he is jealous of). I will, however, suggest that the child and I can make something together that can be taken home, as a way to facilitate that child's ability to hold on to the internal memory of the therapeutic alliance and of the relationship. Children also will sometimes make gifts during the hour, especially cards to express their emotions (or sometimes, lack of them: as when I got a card that said, "I don't like you, but I like your toys").

Today, Ms. Flato brings me another small gift, vegetables from her garden, which I accept with pleasure, thinking (but not telling her) about how I will use them with my supper. As we settle in our chairs,

I think about how to inquire about the meaning of the gift to her, remembering one patient who was insulted by my suggestion that she might be trying to get me to like her more, and the other who was "throwing virgins into the volcano" to keep me from being unhappy with her.

> I believe I know that Ms. Flato's gifts are out of her appreciation of our work, and I don't want to cut off the opportunity for her to be equally *un*appreciative, especially after my absence last week, so I choose to say nothing now. I know that the issue will keep coming up over and over until it is addressed, and I find the "forgivingness" of the therapeutic process reassuring: if I miss something, I'll have other chances to address it as long as the treatment continues.

Ms. Flato begins talking without prompting today, and as I follow her train of thought about her daily life I forget about the gift, which seems not to be significant to her. She begins by remembering when she first came to treatment, when she was feeling completely stuck in a long-term relationship with a man who gave her little or nothing emotionally, and comparing it to some of the very brief relationships she has attempted since. She realizes today that most of the men in her life have been older, and unavailable in some way, either married or uninterested in anything more than occasional sex. We both can recognize the parallel with her father, the prototypical unavailable older man, and she is curious about what purpose that might serve for her. We end the session with that question puzzling both of us, and I hope that next week she will have had some thoughts about it.

No Appointments

In this particular week, after Ms. Flato, I have an unscheduled hour. Since it is Monday, and a Monday after a vacation, I still have mail and messages from the weekend that need to be dealt with: faxes from pharmacies about refilling prescriptions, phone calls that I have not yet been able to return, faxes from insurance companies asking for information about my patients, forms to fill out for insurance companies or for employers about medical leave. It takes me about forty minutes to do the rest of what I can, and I am left with several phone calls where I was not able to contact the person I called and had to leave a message. For lunch, usually salad from a nearby pizzeria, I eat at my desk and read something for fun. Then I chat briefly with my secretaries (Darlene, a part-time secretary, comes in about noon), say hello to Janet (who comes in about 11:00 a.m. and works to 7:00 p.m.), write notes on the patients I saw that morning, and then go out to the front desk for my 1:00 p.m. patient.

Ms. Gantman is a middle-aged woman who had been seeing another psychiatrist for medication management only, but wanted someone that she believed would be "warmer." She told me in our first session that she wanted (needed) to be able to hug me in each session, and today she does so immediately.

> Although many psychiatrists, and most psychotherapists, tend to discourage physical contact with their patients, I do not object to occasional hugs. I am influenced in this by my training as a child psychiatrist, and by my work with young children, who sometimes want to hug you or play games that require physical contact of some sort. As with other issues, I try not to be unthinking about these interactions, and I certainly encourage

the patient to think about what these contacts mean to them, but I generally will not flat out refuse them. For Ms. Gantman, the hug at the beginning and end of each session reminds her that she is noticed and not being judged critically (as she so often judges herself critically), a reassurance that she matters.

With Ms. Gantman, as with other patients I see for both medication and psychotherapy, I find that I need to make a conscious effort to remember to ask about and consider the medication aspect of the treatment. In my usual approach to patients in therapy, I simply wait for them to talk about whatever comes to mind; but sometimes their reaction to medication changes, or possible side effects to medication, does not come to mind until we stand at the end of the session to leave. When I am offering both sorts of service, I try to begin with a "med check" sort of interaction before settling back for the less directive and less focused listening.

Ms. Gantman is somewhat histrionic, and tends to experience all her emotions at a very high intensity, which sometimes makes it hard for her to manage them without "drama." Her depression began in relation to various physical disorders for which her physicians could not find a clear cause and could not find a successful treatment. Much of what she talks about revolves around her disappointment with her various nonpsychiatric physicians as well as other people in her life.

Ms. Gantman immediately tells me today (so quickly that I have no time to ask about her medications) about the frustrations she is having with her accountant about her tax audit. I listen quietly, acknowledging how difficult she finds these struggles, silently wondering what she is hoping for from me and trying to find a thread of recurring ideas in her conversation.

I am not yet clear about what she expects me to do, or how she sees me. She is effusive about how she values her time with me, and sees me as one of the few people who really understands and attends to her feelings, although I don't experience myself as having any deep insight into her life or her emotions. I wonder, as she leaves today, if I will become one of the string of physicians who has disappointed her. Interestingly, on one occasion when I felt I had disappointed her (by not taking her side in a meeting with her husband), she flatly denied having any negative feelings about what I had said; in fact, she denied even disagreeing with what I had said, saying, "You're my doctor, and I trust you!" so I may be relatively safe from becoming one of the "bad" doctors in her eyes.

Ms. Gantman does need help containing her anxiety, and she clearly has a somewhat idealized view of me and of how wonderful I am. Perhaps she just needs to have a "good mother"—a nurturing figure who knows her and cares about her—who will listen and not criticize her. I have so far not succeeded in engaging her in discussing her anxiety as more than a physiological state that keeps her from functioning and likely contributes to her physical problems. I hope eventually to help her recognize that the anxiety is a signal of some internal conflict. If we can reach that point and get a glimpse of what the conflict is, we will be able to explore nonpharmacological means of containing it.

As I listen, it's hard to stay alert for unconscious communications from Ms. Gantman. It feels sometimes as if I hear the same events over and over, and I'm not sure how best to be helpful, although she apparently experiences my listening as positive and accepting. I try as I listen to find ways in which her "episodes" of confusion and problems with balance might be at least partly psychological in origin (as her other doctors believe), but I can't see it. I also don't yet have a clue about the internal struggle that leads to her anxiety. I suspect it has to do with unacknowledged anger, as anxiety so often does (and as it clearly does with Ms. Hatton, my next patient), but I can't be sure. I feel as if I have no idea what is going on, and it's a struggle to wait and listen and not know, without falling into a sort of complaisant state where I let Ms. Gantman talk and then leave without feeling that anything important has happened. I have learned that when I have trouble remaining engaged in this way, it is often because there is a certain lack of relatedness. Perhaps Ms. Gantman wants the *appearance* of being heard more than she truly wants to be heard? Perhaps she is responding to me as some figure from the past that I don't yet know about? Or more likely, a new, better version of some figure from the past: the idealized mother who never criticizes. Since I don't yet understand what is happening between us, I wait and try to remain alert, and to find a way to reconcile her apparent affection for me with the sensation of being emotionally discounted.

Supervision

My 2:00 p.m. appointment is for supervision with Janet, the full-time therapist who works for me. When she began working for me, she moved from a local agency where she had little clinical supervision—most of the supervision was in fact purely administrative, focused on paperwork requirements rather than the clinical work—and she eagerly accepted the idea that we would meet weekly to discuss the cases she was working with. I see this time as a consultation rather than as a true supervision: supervisors have responsibility for the work of their supervisees, where consultants do not, and Janet is fully competent and capable of making her own clinical decisions, so I do not tell her how to proceed with her patients. Talking with her weekly, however, allows me to know what is happening in therapy with the patients for whom I prescribe medication so that I am able to do a better job of collaborating. It also allows Janet and me to compare notes, to be sure that the patients have told me everything I need to know about their medication responses; and it allows Janet and me to help each other to contain, manage, and understand the feelings within ourselves that our work generates. Heidi, the other therapist in the office, also meets with me regularly, but every other week because she is currently part-time.

> Having someone to "vent" to about the strong feelings that come up in doing therapy is extraordinarily valuable, and is one of the reasons that I moved from a private practice with only myself in the office to this setting with two therapists as well as myself. It is a part of the "holding" in the environment, which makes our work possible without burning out. In today's meeting with Janet, there are no particular crisis situations to discuss; instead there has been a significant positive change in one of her patients, who had been stuck for some time, and she and I both are reminded of why the work matters to us and why we keep doing it even when it is hard.

Very Long-Term Therapy

After I meet with Janet, I have another brief break, and at 3:15 I see Ms. Hatton. She has been seeing me weekly for nearly twenty years, and at this point her therapy is primarily supportive. She is a profoundly anxious woman who has been in treatment with me, with both medication and psychotherapy, since shortly after I opened my practice in this area. She is deeply attached to me, and although she lives with her brother, she has few other supports in the area except the other residents in her apartment complex. Many of them have emotional difficulties themselves, as does her brother, and several of them do not hesitate to take advantage of her, asking for money or asking her to give them some of her pills. She has had major difficulties with saying no to anyone since I have known her, and she is usually unable to send those "friends" away when they ask for money or pills without feeling guilty. In today's session she is cheerful and talkative, although somewhat disorganized, recounting the places she has gone for meals with her brother, who also takes financial and emotional advantage of her, and to whom she is unable to say no.

Early in her treatment, Ms. Hatton and I discovered that when she was able to talk about being angry with her brother, her severe anxiety became somewhat less severe. She clearly has difficulty expressing her anger at anyone, except when she is overwhelmed, when she will yell at people (especially her brother) in uncontrolled outbursts. I have never succeeded in getting her to think or to talk about why she cannot be openly angry until she blows up. Occasionally I remind her of what we learned early in her treatment, about the connection between anger and anxiety, but she has not yet been able to take the next step to talk more freely about her anger.

As I listen to Ms. Hatton, sometimes I have trouble remaining alert. Her conversation is rambling, a simple recounting of how she spent her week, with little reflection about her feelings or thoughts. One of my early teachers referred to similar situations as "rent-a-friend" therapy. I sometimes feel that I am doing very little that is useful to Ms. Hatton, and I wonder if I am doing her a disservice by continuing to see her. However, she would be devastated if I asked her to stop coming, and would feel profoundly abandoned, and occasionally there is an opportunity to connect what she is saying with some deeper psychological issues. She herself says that it always helps to see me, that she feels better when she leaves.

With Ms. Hatton, as with Ms. Gantman, I struggle to stay interested and engaged when nothing at all seems to be happening, and again I am reminded that the lack of engagement most likely reflects some difficulty with relatedness. As I listen, I wonder about Ms. Hatton's experience of me. She repeatedly says that we are friends, even though she knows we cannot be social together; and she jokes about finding a way to be in my life outside the office. At times I believe that I may be one of the few people in her life who doesn't take advantage of her in some way. I keep hoping that patient listening in a nonjudgmental way will allow her to find her way to talking more directly about her internal world, the thoughts and feelings that have led her to feel so subordinate to others. I occasionally have a chance to comment on this, and to invite her to tell me her thoughts, but it seldom deepens the level of the conversation. In fact, if I mention her anger, she actively changes the subject and is not able to pursue it with me.

CHAPTER 2: MONDAY

On Mondays, beginning with Ms. Hatton, all of my appointments are standing ones—the same person at the same time on the same day weekly—and I have no breaks. At 4:00 p.m. is Mr. Ignatz, a relatively young man who has been depressed most of his life; he remembers throwing rocks at cars when he was three, and he was hospitalized several times as an adolescent. He first came to see me nine years ago, when he was about thirty. He made significant improvements but still struggled with depression and inability to work consistently in college despite being quite bright. He has since graduated from college—with great difficulty—but continues to want help with his depression. Many of his sessions now are almost entirely silent, and we occasionally talk about what the silence means to him.

> At times it seems to me that he needs to have a space where he is not asked to "produce," to do what the "parent" figure expects, and I remember his childhood memories of sitting trying to do math homework while his parents angrily supervised him.

Today, after perhaps ten minutes of silence, he talks about some relatively superficial interactions at work. It feels to me as if he is not emotionally in the room with me, and when I say so (after about twenty minutes of listening) he agrees that he is not "there," but he is not sure what he is avoiding or why. He is then silent for the rest of the hour, and so am I. I notice today that I am a little grateful for some time without a need for intensely focused attention. When I say we must stop, he gets up and leaves without looking at me, as he always does.

> After he leaves, I reflect on the session and wonder about my grateful acceptance of the "unfocused" time: am I perhaps aware

in the back of my mind that there is a particularly hard issue lurking under the silence? Am I grateful not to have to deal with it? Perhaps later in the week there will be clues about whether this gratitude is specific to Mr. Ignatz, or is my own issue. In the meantime, I reflect briefly about the difference between active conversation and the sort of below-the-surface conversation that is carried by silence in the hour.

After Mr. Ignatz, I go to my computer to meet with Mr. Julian by an online video conferencing application. Mr. Julian is another young man who came to me with a significant academic work inhibition—very different from Mr. Ignatz' work problems—and a very high level of anxiety. He was looking specifically for a psychoanalyst because he knew something about analysis from his graduate work, but he would not have been appropriate for a four-times-a-week treatment. Psychoanalysis is more time-intensive than psychoanalytic psychotherapy—four to five times a week instead of one to three times a week—and is more intensive, at times stirring up very strong feelings. For several reasons, this would not have been possible for Mr. Julian. First of all, he was much too anxious, and he would not have been able to continue functioning in his daily life with the intensity of the emotion that would be stirred up by deeper exploration of his anxiety. He tended to respond to intense anxiety with heavy drinking; and I worried that he would spend all his time drunk and unable to function if we began uncovering his deeper issues too quickly.

Secondly, Mr. Julian lives out of the area and has to travel at least two hours to see me face to face; he would not be able to do it four times a week, and currently can't do it even once a week (which is why we meet online). And finally, he has very poor insurance and would not be able to pay for an analysis. Most of my analytic patients do not pay full fee because most people in Middle America cannot afford the fees and insurance generally will not pay for it; but Mr. Julian was not able to pay full fee even for a single session a week. The combination of what his insurance *did* pay and what he could afford out of pocket was, however, enough for me to be willing to begin with him on a weekly basis, with the possibility that later (as he was less overwhelmed by his anxiety) we could convert the psychotherapy to a psychoanalysis.

As usual, today Mr. Julian talks freely and without giving me a lot of opportunity to make any remarks without interrupting. Today, mostly, he spends a great deal of his time berating himself for being a "loser" and for his supercilious attitude with others, in which he behaves as if he is better than they. This, of course, alienates everybody else, and he is today acutely aware of how lonely he is. He doesn't seem to recognize how his behavior might alienate me or others, or at least keep us from making emotional connections with him.

Over the time that I have been working with Mr. Julian, he has vacillated between looking very groomed and professional—with a buzz cut, wearing preppy clothes—and looking almost derelict, with disheveled hair and an ungroomed beard. He has also vacillated from heavy drinking, telling me stories about being thrown out of a local bar, to intense involvement in his church and Alcoholics Anonymous. The latter activities seem to help provide some needed structure in his life. Currently he has been sober for three months, is attending AA daily, and describes his faith, AA, and me as his primary supports. He seems to be committed to sobriety at this time.

I am pleased for him as he turns his life around, but somewhat skeptical about whether it will last. I point out how he goes to extremes in his behavior (he is now trying to give up smoking, caffeine, and sugar as well as alcohol) rather than finding a balanced way of dealing with the world. We have begun to identify the ways in which he relies on outside structures to "contain" himself—AA and the church—and he is beginning to be more curious about what he finds within himself to help sustain his functioning. We also are just beginning to talk about how he sees himself, and how that self image changes according to whether he is drinking or going to AA, whether he is active at church or stays home watching classic TV for hours. It feels to me today as if we have spent much of the last year simply laying the groundwork for Mr. Julian to begin to look more closely at who he is and how he functions in the world, as if the first year was almost entirely spent in avoiding that reality.

Today I reflect again, as I have before, about how the work with Mr. Julian is affected by being online rather than face-to-face. I have learned that the nature of the therapeutic relationship is changed when you cannot be in the room with your patient. For Mr. Julian it seems to make little difference; and I have wondered in fact if it may be easier for him to talk about very intimate subjects, such as his sex life, when I am not in the same room with him.

After Mr. Julian, I see Kyle, a teenage boy who is significantly depressed and tends to use marijuana to manage his depression, ostensibly with awareness and complicity from his parents (if not out and out permission from them). He is surprisingly self-aware for an adolescent, but is nevertheless focused in a very adolescent way on the opinions of others, feeling that he needs a cool girlfriend to seem cool himself. When he has no girlfriend, he tends to sink into self-depreciation and despair; today he says openly that he does not want to talk about how bad he feels because that just makes it worse, so he talks about politics and history, especially the history of racism and tyranny (for example, Nazi Germany). He and I are both aware that he is avoiding the difficult feelings and that he will not be able to avoid them forever, but he clearly is not able to face them today. It is seldom useful to push someone—

especially an adolescent—to talk about something that he is avoiding, although pointing out the avoidance is helpful; so today I listen and comment on the experiences of individuals such as Kyle in reaction to racism and tyranny, hoping to find a connection there.

As he talks, I wonder how much of his interest in the history of tyranny is because of his tendency to feel that adults are being unreasonable in their expectations, such as the requirement that he attend school regularly.

Although Kyle's parents are aware of his marijuana use, I have not spoken to them about it. They are unusually willing to allow Kyle to have the "space" to work things out on his own, with my help, and have never asked to speak with me.

My guiding principle with adolescents and children is that they need a space where they can talk about whatever is going on in their life without fear of being "turned in," so I do not tell their parents what is happening in their therapy unless it is a specific safety issue, such as suicidal thoughts or threats to harm others. I will take telephone calls from family and will listen to whatever they want me to know about the child or adolescent, but I will not tell them anything without my patient's permission. In the case of adolescents, this stance is supported by state law, which requires permission to release information even to parents for anyone over fourteen. For children, I talk with parents about this at the beginning of therapy and explain the rationale. Many (but not all) therapists work the same way with children and their families; for me, it represents my attempt to be for these children the "nonintrusive" or "nonimpinging" therapist that Winnicott describes as crucial for growth of the self.

At the end of my day, at 7:30 in the evening, I have another online session, this time with Ms. Leakman, a young woman who first saw me while a student at a local college. She had been a sports star in high school until the onset of fibromyalgia, and her reaction to the loss of her expected future in sports was significant depression and self-hatred. Therapy in high school had helped her stop cutting herself and had eliminated her suicidal thoughts, but when she came to college she still struggled with an inability to feel that she could be good at anything else. She also shared concerns about knowing who she was and knowing that she was good enough. Many late adolescents and young adults have some struggles with identity and with being able to feel good about themselves, to feel capable and competent, but for Ms. Leakman this was exacerbated by the loss of her expected successes in sports.

Ms. Leakman was able to get through college with minimal difficulties, although she often brought her struggles to me in weekly psychotherapy. When she graduated and returned to her parents' home in a large urban area and found a job in that area, she opted to continue in weekly therapy with me via Skype. In today's session, she talks about the demanding job she is working at and her drive to perform and to show everyone—including herself—that she can be special and above average even though she cannot be a sports star. She frequently compares herself to her brilliant brother, who has just finished law school, and feels she is "good enough" but not great—which of course means she is not good enough for herself. She sees the patterns in her life of feeling not good enough and of being driven to prove that she can be the best; she also recognizes the need to balance her driven achievements with something that allows relaxation and activities other than work. Our conversations tend to move back and forth among work, her leisure activities, and her attempts to continue to be satisfied with her achievements.

After I sign offline with Ms. Leakman, I am quite tired. I take my purse and e-tablet (where I do most of my reading these days), lock up the office and turn out the lights, and go home. I am the last one out of the office building, and walking out through a dark lobby (because everyone else left an hour earlier) to my lonely car feels like a great relief. Once I am home, I will have supper, read for a few hours, and then go to bed.

Chapter 3

Tuesday

Tuesday morning, I again arrive just before 8:00 a.m. and check for messages (this time only one, a prescription request that came in overnight). After a trip to the file room to pull the charts I will need for the day, I sit to play solitaire with my first cup of coffee, chatting with Patty about her grandchildren. Ms. Austin is my first patient of the day, and when she arrives about five minutes late (as is usual for her), I'm happy to get started.

Ms. Austin

Ms. Austin is very heavy and wears only dresses, with fashionable scarves that she describes as her "trademark." Today she is wearing a dress I have not seen before, similar to the style of dresses that I wear; it has more color than her usual dark clothes, and I wonder about her changing tastes. She has commented herself on how her taste in clothes is changing as she watches how I dress.

> As I walk down the curving hall after Ms. Austin, carrying my coffee, I begin thinking about some of the details of our work together. She missed the last session prior to my vacation unexpectedly because she was ill, and then she cancelled yesterday because she was presenting at a professional conference. I think, "Maybe she's showing me that she doesn't have to worry about my going away because she can go away first and come back later, so it's in her control and not mine." I wonder if she will say anything about the missed sessions; and I remember other conversations about the possible meanings of her chronic lateness. She says it's just because she has trouble getting up in the morning, even though she's never late to professional appointments. I suspect myself, and have suggested but not insisted to her, that she is "testing" to see how I react when she's not a "good patient" (or at least not doing what she thinks I expect). Ms. Austin's wish to please me, to be closer to me, even to be more like me, is something that we both are aware of but have not yet spoken about more than in passing. It is clear, though, that before she eventually finishes her work with me this will need to come into focus and be understood fully.

Ms. Austin sits on the couch with her "go-cup" of coffee, adjusts her scarf, and begins talking while sitting up. The shared experience of coffee adds a note of friendship, more than purely professional relatedness, to our time together. After she finishes the coffee she will lie down on the couch, and sometimes she takes longer with the coffee if she wants to be able to see my face and read my expression. We both know that when she is trying to avoid a particular topic she will sit up longer. Today she begins with talking about her current reading, which lately has been about psychoanalysis and some of the early psychoanalysts: "I've been reading the Khan book." She's referring to *False Self: The Life of Masud Khan* (2006), by Linda Hopkins; Khan was a psychoanalyst in the 1950s and 1960s, prominent in Britain at a time when most of today's famous names were his colleagues and were establishing their reputations. It is well known that Khan was considered brilliant, but that toward the end of his career he became very erratic, perhaps psychotic, and was known for having sex with his female patients.

> I am startled, both at Ms. Austin's reading and at her eagerness to talk about it, because she read about psychoanalysis early in her analysis but did not talk about it then. This is the first time she has told me much about what she is reading, though she often mentions titles. This book was not one I have read yet and have not been particularly interested in before, in part because of Masud Khan's reputation as quite disturbed.

Ms. Austin does not talk about Khan himself, but about how "the early analysts seemed to practice very differently than today, much more like a joint project than like a doctor-patient relationship."

"I'm not sure what you mean," I say, and she responds that she tends to think of her analysis as me treating her rather than as the two of us doing something together.

> I am taken aback at this because my therapeutic "style" tends to be quite personal. Perhaps it relates to having trained as a child

71

psychoanalyst, but being distant and formal does not work for me.

It surprised Ms. Austin to read about the analysts feeling "personally involved," learning about themselves and changing as a result, as described in "the Khan book." She doesn't see me as personally involved in that way, but "as kind of an omniscient narrator," guiding the treatment. When I suggest, "So I have all the power here, and you have none?" she agrees.

"Modern theories of psychoanalysis emphasize boundaries and restrictions," she continues, making it clear that "boundaries" imply an emotional distance. Winnicott (Khan's analyst) and other analysts of the time, however, seem not as "clinically distant" to her.

I think silently, *She might be worried that I'm too distant, that I don't care about her like Winnicott cared. I wonder if my vacation felt like I abandoned her.* I also notice, on the edge of my thoughts, a new interest in the book, as Winnicott is one of my professional "heroes." My own understanding of the holding environment, and the need to be careful to allow the analysand space to become herself, not to intrude one's own views, is grounded in Winnicott's thinking.

What I say is, "Well, we certainly know more about boundaries now than the early analysts."

She goes on to say, "Those people shared a lot more about themselves with their patients than analysts now. You let me know more about you than a lot of therapists, but still not very much."

At the periphery of my thoughts, almost not consciously, I know that Ms. Austin's bringing up this subject means that something is "hot" in the transference, that she has feelings about me and our relationship that she cannot yet talk about openly. Because every relationship we have reflects our internal view of the world and of what we expect from relationships, we can learn a great deal about the patient's view of the world by observing how the analytic relationship develops. Exploring the transference is a particularly powerful way of looking at this because it is so immediate. At this point in the session, however, I do not comment on knowing that something is "hot" because I am engaged in listening to the content of what Ms. Austin is telling me, hoping that she will say more about her view of me. For Ms. Austin, discussion of the relationship with me often gets lost in material about her daily life, and I am not yet sure if this is active avoidance of that material, so I wait.

I say, "The most modern theories emphasize intersubjectivity, the idea that the therapeutic relationship is between two people and that both are changed by it. I have always believed that in a really good analysis, I will inevitably be different at the end of it."

Thinking about this interchange now, I know that I responded intellectually rather than addressing my suspicion about her wanting me to care, even though my training and experience tell me that it would likely move us *away* from the important feelings rather than toward them. I believe now that I was uncomfortable, without even recognizing it in myself, about her wish for me to be more personal. Many of the early analysts—including Masud

Khan in his later life—were wildly inappropriate (by current standards) in some of their actions, and I think I was afraid of being drawn into similar behaviors. Because Ms. Austin wants so badly to be loved by others, she is vulnerable to inappropriate relationships; and in fact in high school she was seduced by a teacher, and in college was seduced by her first psychotherapist. Although those relationships are long ago, and she would say that she no longer would allow such things to happen, I suspect (then unconsciously, now consciously) that she wants to have an intimate—and inappropriate—relationship with me. I did not then, of course, say any of this to Ms. Austin, because I was busy myself avoiding the issue by teaching her instead of looking for the unconscious content of her material. I do not realize my own pattern of avoidance by intellectualization until Ms. Austin has left the room for the day.

Ms. Austin is silent for a moment and then says, "We talk a lot about how we can't go out to lunch together or things like that, but I still don't really understand why. It's hard for me to be open enough, as if something is holding me back. It's like there's a little piece of me that's afraid of being rejected, even though you've given me no reason. If there are some places I can't go in here, how can I feel safe?"

I am silent for a moment, and then say, "There are no places *you* can't go; the rules are for *me.*"

I remember fleetingly other patients who have tried to cross that social boundary, and what I learned from them about how to understand and verbalize the reasons for the boundary. Over the years there have been several patients who wanted a social relationship, a friendship, over and above the therapeutic relationship that we had established. As I try to understand this wish each time, and try to explain why it is not possible, I have to clarify for myself exactly why it is not possible, aside from the simple "thou shalt not" that almost everyone knows about. In my training, my teachers were very clear that such relationships are not possible, that boundaries are critical, and that a social relationship represents a boundary violation; but they never explained why that was true in a way that I could use with patients. What I finally came to is the understanding that a friendship is balanced and reciprocal. If I am angry or upset, I want my friend to listen to me and to comfort me, but a therapeutic relationship is essentially one-sided. In the forty-five minutes I spend with each patient on any given day, it is my job to set aside my own feelings and needs as much as possible to focus on the patient's feelings and needs. I may not ask the patient to meet my needs, to take care of me, except as the work itself meets my emotional needs (and, of course, it is how I make a living). If I am stressed or upset, I must somehow set that aside until my patient has left; and if I am not able to do so, perhaps I need to cancel appointments until I can.

Frame of Therapy

Much of the frame of therapy—the practical arrangements that determine when and how often and for how long you meet, what sort of contact you have outside the therapy hour, what the fee is, how the fee is paid—serves a double purpose. It serves to provide a structure that the patient can both shelter in and fight against ("What a relief! It's time for my session so I can get this off my chest!" or "Oh, good, it's time to stop now so I don't have to think about this stuff right now") as she uses the safe space of the consulting room to face the things she can't otherwise face. But the frame also contains and holds the therapist, limiting unconsidered or unwise actions until we can think them through; it reassures us that we don't have to experience the intolerable rage or overwhelming grief or annihilating anxiety longer than the end of the hour.

Being able to cancel sessions when we ourselves feel personally overwhelmed allows us to use the formal structure of the treatment to contain the intense feelings of the patient. This in turn makes it possible for us to continue being the *patient's* container, to provide the safe space within which they explore their own selves. If we give up the frame that contains us, we will not be able to be the container for our patients.

After clarifying that the rules are for me, not for Ms. Austin, I ask how she thinks about the "rule" that we can't be friends, and she cannot find any reason for it. I say, "For me, the basic reason is that a friendship is reciprocal, and this relationship is not. If we were friends, then when I was having a bad day I'd want to tell you about that, instead of listening to you and trying to understand you. For the forty-five minutes you're here, you're my first priority. I set my own stuff aside so I can make a space that allows you to find yourself."

She thinks about it, and then says, "I just have the feeling I'm not doing it right ... in the Khan book, it's about all the weird things people do. They're so regressed and crazy."

"Do you think you're not crazy enough?"

She laughs, and agrees; and then we have to stop.

After Ms. Austin leaves, I wish that we had had time to talk more about this issue. Her experiences with her previous therapist— and even more with her high school teacher—have complicated her current relationships in many ways. She wants very badly to be loved, and so is vulnerable to being taken advantage of; and those early experiences make intimacy with authority figures (such as a therapist) both very familiar and alarming. I think that understanding how egregiously her first therapist had transgressed would help to lessen her guilt and shame about that incident. I also think that perhaps she believes I am not as "personal" with her as Winnicott had been in his work with Khan because she is not a "good enough patient"; and I know that understanding the issue more clearly would help her to know that I am not rejecting her. I am resigned to waiting until the issue comes up again, as it certainly will, and again remember that important issues come up repeatedly until we address them.

Interlude

I turn on the overhead lights in my consulting room that are off when someone is using the couch, and then I have time to get another cup of coffee before moving to my computer for a session online with a patient in China. I have for some years been a faculty member for the China-American Psychoanalytic Alliance, a group that provides formal training in psychoanalytic psychotherapy for Chinese students, which includes two years of classes and individual supervision with psychoanalysts throughout the world. All the work is conducted in English, and the students are carefully screened for their English proficiency. Prior to the establishment of CAPA, the only training available for Chinese professionals in psychoanalytic psychotherapy was in two-to-five-day workshops in the country, or residence outside the country for a training program. I have been involved with CAPA since its founding in about 2008, providing weekly supervision for two students, and most years teaching a continuing case conference weekly. CAPA also offers the opportunity for individual psychotherapy or psychoanalysis via teleconferencing, since having one's own therapy is an important part of becoming a good therapist.

Ms. Ma, the Chinese patient I speak with at 9:00 a.m. on Tuesdays, has finished her CAPA training and is currently in practice in China. I have learned a great deal about establishing a therapeutic relationship from the work online with Ms. Ma and my previous CAPA patient. I know that it takes longer for me to feel truly "connected" with patients on the internet, to feel comfortable in the electronic relationship; and the occasional problems with internet service change the back-and-forth of the conversation. Ms. Ma in particular often asks that I write down what I am saying, and "instant message" it so that she can be sure she understands me. Luckily I type fairly fast, so it doesn't interrupt the flow of the conversation much.

Using the Internet

When I meet with Ms. Ma, I am acutely aware of the difficulties in the electronic interchange. Early in her treatment we had great difficulty in maintaining clear connections, and often I felt I was missing more than half of what she was saying. I tolerated the problems for some time, hoping they would improve as I upgraded the processing power of my computer, but finally I let Ms. Ma know that I felt I was not doing her a service by continuing to meet with her when I could not understand what she was saying. I suggested that a new therapist might have better internet service, with a better connection. She was quite upset, and told me that she felt as if I was abandoning her; she had assumed that my silence was "patiently listening" rather than not being able to respond because I did not understand, and she had become attached to me in part because she saw me as so patient and accepting. I agreed to continue working with her, and eventually the connection improved for unknown reasons; but each time we have trouble hearing each other, I am reminded of this experience.

> Recently I have been asking myself, "If just listening silently is enough, why do we need even to say anything? What do I have to offer that a computer can't do?" The answer, of course, is that our patients need to know not only that we are silently present, but also that we are in fact listening actively and are engaged in their story. Telling one's story to a computer is *not* the same as telling it to a live, engaged human being. It is important to be able to maintain silence, to patiently listen, but to be engaged and able to respond when needed.

Today Ms. Ma is relatively happy; there have been some positive developments at work that have allowed her to feel more successful than she sometimes does, and she spends the hour mostly describing those events. She is always thoughtful and self-reflective, and often I need to do very little but offer remarks that remind her of things she has understood in the past, or that let her know I understand her emotional reactions to her life.

> As I listen to Ms. Ma, I remember Winnicott's remarks about the uses of silence. He says that "I seldom make an interpretation

and the analysis proceeds best on the basis of my saying nothing at all" (Winnicott 1965b, 85). He goes on to assert, "One of the purposes of interpreting is to establish the limits of the analyst's understanding. The basis for *not* interpreting" (italics mine) "and in fact not making any sound at all is the theoretical assumption that the analyst really does know what is going on." This reflects his strong belief that given a proper facilitating environment (1960), the patient and the patient's unconscious processes will take the treatment where it needs to go, and the analyst need only trust the process and, for the most part, keep her mouth shut.

Uses of Theory

To do this—to trust the process and keep my mouth shut—I need to remain solidly grounded in the theory of my work. In the hour with the patient, I seldom think about theory except in passing, as my associations touch on something I have read or was taught. But without theory, I would be overwhelmed by the lack of order and the apparent meaninglessness of the patient's associations until we find that meaning together. With theory, I can contain my anxiety about not yet understanding my patient, can remember that even the most disturbed patients are not irredeemably crazy, but are simply distressed and overwhelmed. With this thought, listening to Ms. Ma, my mind goes to the first individual I saw with multiple personality disorder (now called dissociative identity disorder). Early in this woman's treatment, I spent some time feeling very frightened about how disturbed she was, and wondering if I would be able to help her, feeling that I was "in over my head." Once I realized that she was experiencing dissociative identity disorder, my reaction was more along the lines of, "Oh, well, that's just what multiples do … just hang on, and you can deal with it with her along the way."

Theory does help us to contain our anxiety, and to tolerate not knowing about the patient in order to allow the patient to find himself. Casement (1991, 8) quotes Bion as saying, "In every consulting room there ought to be two rather frightened people; the patient and the psycho-analyst. If they are not, one wonders why they are bothering to find out what everyone knows."

Being Surprised

It is also, however, important not to let theory inhibit us or make us decide prematurely that we understand what is going on rather than letting the patient lead us to new and perhaps unfamiliar material. Our task is to perturb the ordered way that the patient experiences the world, allowing temporary discomfort and disorganization for the sake of the opportunity it opens for change.

To do this, we must also perturb the order *we* experience. We may believe we can, based on previous similar interactions, predict where our patient is going in his conversation, but we should not go there prematurely. Rather, we need to leave the door open to be surprised. My experience is that in any good therapy there is at least one surprise; and if I am never surprised by my patient, I am missing something. There are commonalities and similarities among all of us—"We are all more simply human than otherwise" (Harry Stack Sullivan)—but we are all also different. When we can allow ourselves the freedom to not know what is going on at first so that later we can be surprised, we find the differences that make our patients more truly themselves.

As I write this, I wonder how Ms. Ma has surprised me, or if I am missing something in her treatment. The surprise, I think, was discovering that what I thought was emotional absence was felt by her as patient listening. But I still do not feel I understand how that gap between my experience and hers began, or how it was bridged.

I frequently think of how often *my* experience in, and understanding of, the therapeutic relationship is radically different from the *patient's* experience in and understanding of the relationship, and I remind myself always to ask, never to assume that I know what the patient is thinking or feeling.

After Ms. Ma and I end our time together, I again have a brief break. This time I use the time to prepare as best I can for my next patient, Ms. Nevill, who comes only once a month. I take a moment to remember the early days of her treatment, when she was overwhelmed by her anxiety, to the point that she could not sit for more than a few minutes, and talked nonstop about herself and her feelings. Early in the treatment I felt deluged by her words, drowning in them, and was unable to make sense of them because of her disorganization and the rush from topic to topic. I had to remind myself frequently—and I remind myself again today—that it is not my job to make people change their behavior; rather, it is my job to understand why they behave as they do, and try to help them understand it also, so that they can change it if they wish.

Over several years Ms. Nevill has slowly become less anxious and overwhelmed, and she is now able to be self-reflective, to stop and take time to think things through, and to make some very positive changes in her life. She is less frantic than when I first met her, is able to recognize some of the issues in her life that fueled the anxiety, and can step back from doing things that will make it worse. Ms. Nevill would, I believe, benefit from more frequent sessions, but she has chosen to use her time to build her new life rather than to continue more intensive therapeutic work. I am clear that she does a fair amount of avoidance by simply refusing to think about things, but the avoidance is no longer as disruptive and destructive as when I first met her. Today, for the first time, she remarks on having realized how dependent she was on her parents when she first came into treatment; and she expresses her pride at having become significantly more independent.

I wonder at times if I need to push more for Ms. Nevill to recognize the ways in which she uses activity to keep herself from thinking about herself. When I have tried in the past, she has at times missed appointments, or fallen into a crisis in her life that demanded our focus on the crisis rather than on background patterns of behavior. I have had to remind myself yet again that it is not my job to change her behavior, but to help her understand. I will still say what I think, but it is quite clear that her defenses—the ways in which she represses and avoids thinking about uncomfortable issues—are very effective, and she will not face the uncomfortable issues until she is ready, no matter what I do. So I tolerate the waiting, say what I can when she is able to hear, and watch as she slowly becomes more comfortable with herself. I must often remind myself to notice how she is slowly changing, so that I can tolerate the waiting; at times I find myself dreading the time with Ms. Nevill because I know that I am likely to feel almost superfluous as she talks nonstop, convincing herself that she is doing so well that she does not need more frequent therapy sessions. Interestingly, these days I don't feel disengaged and bored as often as I would have at times early in her treatment. This suggests to me that Ms. Nevill is herself more engaged in the therapeutic interaction, as my own boredom is often (but not always) a reaction to the patient's lack of engagement.

Diagnostic Evaluation

After Ms. Nevill leaves, I have an appointment for a "one-time evaluation" with a young man sent over by Juvenile Probation. Many of the adolescents who end up on probation are young people who have mental health issues, and not infrequently their delinquent behavior is their way of dealing with their emotional issues. Since those delinquent behaviors led ultimately to their arrest, it seems likely that they have not found a way to deal successfully with those mental health issues. My task for Probation is to offer an opinion about diagnosis and appropriate interventions, without myself taking on the treatment of these adolescents. Today I will see the adolescent; later in the week I will review all the written records I have received, talk with parents by phone if possible, and create a written report with my diagnostic impressions and my recommendations.

These evaluations illustrate to me most clearly the differences between how I think about diagnosis and treatment and how much of the rest of the world thinks about it. I do not generally find that a diagnostic label—depression, or generalized anxiety disorder, or bipolar disorder—is helpful in understanding why an individual does things the way he does. It is a shorthand we use for communicating with other professionals, but it is only descriptive, not at all explanatory. In adolescents, this is particularly true: given three adolescents, all of whom are truant, oppositional, talking back to parents, and having problems with anger management, one will be depressed, one may be anxious and trying to be "tough," and one may be psychotic (hearing and seeing things). The behaviors are the same, and our current diagnostic categories would tend to assign similar diagnoses to each; but the underlying causes of the behaviors are different.

In thinking about treatment or other interventions, I also take a somewhat different approach to identifying the goals of treatment. The juvenile justice system (as well as many therapists) sees behavior change as the ultimate goal. In my experience, though, sometimes the behavior does not change with therapy even though the feelings that accompany the behaviors change profoundly, so that the individual is more content and less angry or depressed. Sometimes the behaviors do not change, but the individual can explain why the behaviors make sense; an example would be the child who runs away from home who ultimately reveals in treatment that she is being abused in the home and has no other way to be safe. In the evaluation today, as in everything I do, I try to keep both goals—behavior change and addressing the hidden causes of the behavior—in mind for my recommendations.

Family Therapy in Pieces

After the adolescent boy from Juvenile Probation leaves, I see Ms. O'Malley, who is working with me in individual psychotherapy about her depression and anxiety. Her case is unusual, however, because her two sons are also seen in my office, and I have in the past seen her husband for medication.

It is generally considered a bad idea for the same mental health professional to see multiple family members because there tends to be some conflict of interest. In particular, I have found that when I see more than one family member for therapy, even briefly, inevitably at least one person in the family will start to worry about whether I am telling other family members what they are saying to me. It feels very unsafe to talk about being angry with your mother, or your brother, if you think your therapist will tell the other person that you are angry. I have several families in my practice, however, where I have violated that unwritten rule for what seem to me to be good reasons. In the case of Ms. O'Malley, her sons came into treatment for anxiety and attention deficit hyperactivity disorder some years ago; each is seeing one of the two therapists in the office, and I see each for medication. I also see her husband for medication management, and he is in therapy outside of this office. Knowing about the family constellation, and being able to talk with both therapists about how the boys are doing, has been quite helpful in my work with the kids. Ideally I would also have occasional conversations with father's therapist, but it is much more difficult to do so with outside therapists. These days I will see multiple family members for medication management, but will not generally see two members of the same family in individual psychotherapy.

Most recently, Ms. O'Malley called me to say that she was feeling overwhelmed and depressed. I met with her about the possibility of medication, and we agreed that she would benefit from the opportunity also to talk about her life stresses and to understand the patterns in how she copes. She had been involved in therapy elsewhere, but when her insurance changed it would not pay for services from her then-therapist, and she could not afford to pay out of pocket. She then began treatment with me.

Ms. O'Malley began her work with me by announcing that she was "surrounded with men who all need to be mothered:" her sons, her husband, her boss. Because I knew about her history with her sons and her husband, I was able to appreciate the essential reality of this more poignantly than I might have otherwise, and I found myself less likely to challenge her perceptions. It is of course true that we want to focus on the patient's internal reality, not on external reality. In Ms. O'Malley's case, I did not start by wondering about why she was reacting so strongly to an "average expectable" home environment (as I might have with someone else), but I wondered about how she had managed to replicate so well the circumstances of her childhood home, where she was expected and required to put everyone else's needs ahead of her own. I was aware that my own occasional exasperation with her husband's passivity and lack of engagement in his own therapy was shaping my responses to Ms. O'Malley in part, and I tried to be careful about keeping that in check as I listened to her exasperation and feeling of being burdened.

I have had similar experiences over the years, seeing one family member for therapy and others (who are in therapy with

Janet or Heidi in my office) only for medication, and I have come to think of this work as a sort of "family therapy in pieces." Each member of the family influences what happens with the others; and individual therapy also has a family impact because the individual patient interacts with others in the family. It feels appropriate to me to work in this way as long as the other therapists and I are mindful of the boundaries, and as long as we work to keep all of the individual therapies solidly grounded in the family context. We also are careful not to talk with each other about details of the individual sessions, but to share only thoughts about the family patterns of interactions.

I have also found it hard to refuse to do this sort of work over my years in this small community, even though my training suggests that it may not be ideal. It seems to me that this situation makes it clear why "rules" are truly guidelines, not rules that cannot be broken: to flexibly respond to the needs of the individual patient, one must be ready to step outside the usual practice. It is easier to just "follow the rules," but doing so makes it impossible to truly individualize the treatment.

When one family member has been in treatment with a good outcome, it seems natural that when another family member has difficulties he or she would want to return to the same place for help. Some families have told me that if they could not see me, they would not see anyone because they didn't trust anybody else. Although I try, in the course of treatment, to address this general distrust and to suggest that other professionals can be trusted, I am not willing to deny them the help they need. When I agree to such nontraditional arrangements, I try to be as clear as possible about boundaries and to remain always mindful about the complications of the model, about the good reasons for the more traditional approach, so as to sidestep the problems that those "rules" are intended to avoid.

Ms. O'Malley had a very positive response to the medication we used, and she has also chosen to continue in psychotherapy as we talk about how she allows herself to be co-opted as "handmaiden" to the men in her life, and how that connects to her sense, dating back to her childhood, of not being valued. In today's session she is feeling less taken advantage of and more able to stand up for her own needs with others, so when she leaves I am feeling positive and like I am making a difference for her.

Long-Term Follow-Up

After Ms. O'Malley, I have an appointment with Paige, a young woman I saw several times a week for about three years, until she went away to college at eighteen. When I go out to the waiting room, I see an attractive young woman who is clearly more mature than the slightly nerdy, awkward girl I remember. She comes into my office and sits without speaking. Unlike my usual practice, I begin the conversation, saying that I was surprised she had called for an appointment, since she had hated seeing me so much. She responds, with a sly smile, "I wanted to yell at someone, and I didn't want to yell at my roommate, and I didn't want to yell at my family, but I knew I could yell at you."

This is absolutely congruent with the Paige I knew: she saw me three times a week for three years as a young teenager without ever saying anything positive, spending most of her time criticizing my tacky clothes, my ugly office furniture, my hair, my personality. Despite her criticisms and her verbalized scorn for me, however, she never missed an appointment and was never late. On one occasion, when I had cancelled, she came anyway. In the next session, she said, "I know what you're going to say. You're going to say I *wanted* to be here, but I didn't! I just forgot!" She was relentless in her angry and rejecting attitude. I listened, accepted the criticism and scorn (often with some amusement, as she was quite creative in her insults), and when I was able offered thoughts about what her internal psychological conflicts might be. She never, as far as I can remember, agreed with any of my thoughts about her internal world, but she occasionally would in later sessions refer to them as if we both knew they were true.

For a long time, I have thought about what might have been helpful for Paige in her treatment. She clearly did benefit from it: she became noticeably less angry with family and friends, the suicidal thoughts that brought her into treatment disappeared, and she was able finally to go off to college and succeed. The best I can say is that it was helpful to Paige to have someone who could tolerate her anger and survive it without retaliation. Donald Winnicott has described the need for the analyst to survive the patient's aggression without being angry or retaliating as a way for the patient to come to terms with and learn to contain his or her own aggression (Rodman, 181). I suppose that with Paige I was the survivor that could allow her to be angry without striking back. As Casement (1991, 178) says about a similar patient, "When, in the end, the patient was able to realize I had continued to survive her attacks upon the [therapy], and upon me, she began to discover it was safe for her to become more fully alive in herself."

When Paige began in treatment with me, she had been cutting herself, thinking about suicide (by swallowing batteries so the battery acid would kill her), and doing unusual things like showering in a bathing suit because she could not tolerate being nude even for bathing. By the end of her treatment, none of these things were happening. In the course of her treatment, I often had to face the conflict between my hopes for behavior change in Paige and the reality that successful treatment brings change in the internal world, not primarily in external behavior. The individual who comes into treatment throwing up so that she cannot go to school may, at the end of a successful treatment, still not be going to school, but now because she flatly refuses rather than because she uses bodily symptoms to make it impossible. The transformation of unconscious wishes not to go to school into conscious anger about being coerced to go is a long step toward a more healthy way of dealing with the external world.

For Paige, the attacks on herself by self-harm and suicide attempts turned into an open expression of how angry she was at people and things in the outside world. She was able to contain that anger, in part, by making me the recipient in her internal world of much of the anger, so that the important people in her external world could be safe from it. As Casement tells us (1991, 269–270), "The analytic good object … is someone who survives being treated as the bad object," who doesn't collapse or leave or retaliate. For Paige, because I was able to survive her anger without retaliating, collapsing, or rejecting her, she could learn to manage it both internally and externally.

Paige clearly does not want anything from me today except to "have someone to yell at," so I listen to her update on her life, which is critical of me but not as relentlessly as previously. After she leaves, I have a few minutes during which I share with Janet my pleasure and amusement at having been allowed to see Paige's improvement (which may be another reason for her coming back to see me: to show me what we achieved without having to admit it to me). Then I see Mr. Ignatz for his second appointment of the week.

Dealing with Silence

Today Mr. Ignatz is again silent for the first ten or fifteen minutes, and as I wait for him to decide how to begin I think about how my own attitude toward silence has changed over the years.

> In my first years of practice, in training and immediately after, I was always uncomfortable with long silences, and supervisors often would remind me that the analyst should do significantly less talking than the patient. One supervisor told me that after a long silence, the individual who speaks first is usually the more anxious of the pair, and reminded me that I needed to be less anxious than the patient in order to provide the "holding" and containment that my patients needed and deserved. With Mr. Ignatz, I have learned that lesson thoroughly; and sometimes now I wonder about how to discern when remaining silent is truly "holding" and when it is colluding with the patient's avoidance (since one of the basic rules for the analyst is—usually—to not collude with defenses such as avoidance). Mr. Ignatz talks about the meaning of his silence spontaneously enough, and often enough, that I don't believe it is primarily avoidance, but that it is a communication of a profound need on his part; and I continue trying to figure out what need he is communicating. Perhaps as Winnicott has suggested (1965a), it is because there is

a core to the personality that must remain isolate, "permanently non-communicating, permanently unknown, in fact unfound." For this core of the self, silence is itself a communication: a communication of the ability to be "alone in the presence of another" (Winnicott 1965b) without withdrawing, the capacity to know and be comfortable with oneself.

Reverie

I also have learned to attend to my own thoughts during these long silences, allowing what we call my *reverie* to come to the forefront. *Reverie* is a term that all analysts use freely but that few of us can define. Freud calls it "evenly hovering attention"; Wilfred Bion (1962, 34-36) understands it as the state of mind that allows one to be unconsciously receptive to the other, allowing the other to experience his or her unconscious desires and fears in relation to the analyst rather than to the important objects from early life (that is, reverie allows therapists to accept the transference projections from their patients, to feel at least temporarily as if we are in fact how the patient sees us). Thomas Ogden suggests that reverie is a *shared* state of being, which "invokes (a partial) giving over of one's separate individuality to a third subject, a subject that is neither analyst or analysand, but a third subjectivity unconsciously generated by the analytic pair." Attempts to describe reverie often slide into this sort of evocative language that seems to mean something profound but is almost impossible to describe clearly.

During the analytic hour, as we listen to our patient's wandering thoughts, we are also, and simultaneously, attending to our own wandering thoughts: the random and not-so-random ideas that pass through the edges of our awareness and that seldom take clear shape but lead us to fleeting ideas and associations about our patient's remarks. When we can attend simultaneously to the explicit content of what is being said and to our own associations, we may have clues about the latent content of our patient's speech: the unconscious meaning, the connections to past thoughts and experiences. It is my reverie— touching on things my patient has said to me, things other patients have said, things I've read, current events, daydreams, fantasies, bodily sensations—that allows me to listen and make connections for the patient, that frees my unconscious processes to meet his unconscious processes in the "analytic third" that Ogden describes, and to generate new understandings. As I wait for Mr. Ignatz to feel free enough to speak out loud, I pursue these connections in my own mind.

After about fifteen minutes, Mr. Ignatz begins to talk about his own thoughts about the silence. He reminds himself that *his* basic rule is to say whatever comes to his mind as best he can without censoring himself; and that he doesn't have to worry about what he's accomplishing, he just has to trust the analytic process and say whatever comes to mind, and we will eventually get somewhere.

This profound trust in the analytic process is somewhat discomfiting to me, although I share it. I can tell myself, and tell others when I teach, to "trust the process," that you don't always need to understand what is happening for it to happen, that you can figure out later why the process worked. I know from my training and my experience that it is the relationship, and the provision of the holding space for the patient, that allows patients like Mr. Ignatz to find their way to do what they need to heal themselves. But in my heart of hearts—quite in opposition to my training and my consciously held beliefs—I still have a sneaking suspicion that as the doctor I am supposed to "do something" (as Ms. Austin expects), and that if I don't my patient will suffer.

I have lately been reading more of Winnicott's work about psychoanalysis, and his belief that interpretation—providing a conscious understanding of unconscious processes—is *not* what is most helpful for people with profound character-based symptoms such as those Mr. Ignatz presents. Winnicott distinguishes "psychoneuroses" (disorders with symptoms that originate in unconscious mental conflicts) from what he calls "madness," or psychosis as the early British analysts used the term (not at all what we mean by that term today). For the early British analysts, psychosis referred to disorders that arose from existential or character-based distortions of early development, resulting in "false self" positions, where one never is able to feel solidly real. Sometimes it seems to me that many of the people we see in the early twenty-first century for psychotherapy are struggling with similar "false self" structures.

Winnicott, I believe, would be quite clear that the appropriate approach for Mr. Ignatz would be to create an environment in which he was "contained and experienced," much as the mother "contains and experiences" the infant by soothing the infant's distress, calming the infant's tantrums, and seeing the infant as precious and valuable. Mother's soothing and containment helps the infant develop the capacity to self-soothe and self-integrate, by reflecting back the child's expression of his/her internal state ("Oh, you're so angry! I'm sorry I was late with your bottle!"). Until now, commenting on what was happening would most likely have diverted Mr. Ignatz from the experience, and would not have been helpful. I have continued to wait for the moment when we might be able to talk about how important it is to him for me to allow the silence without exasperation or frustration, and how he could find himself in that experience. Perhaps the gratitude I felt on Monday at being able to be silent with him myself is what allows me to not be exasperated or frustrated about the silence.

Reflecting on these issues, and on what Winnicott might say about Mr. Ignatz, allows me to be silent and to wait for his readiness to share his current thoughts and feelings with me. After some minutes, I say, "I think it's a new experience for you to have someone who most of the time is trying to understand what you need, instead of just telling you what to do." He says, "Yes, it is," and then falls silent again. After another ten minutes of silence—this time much less uncomfortable—the hour is up, and he leaves.

In that last ten minutes of silence, I wonder what will happen in Mr. Ignatz's next session. We know from experience that when an interpretation—a suggestion about the unconscious meaning of a behavior—is correct, it often results in the patient bringing in new memories or new material about his internal world. Perhaps in our next session Mr. Ignatz will be able to give up some of the silence and tell me more about his internal world.

Sharing My Work with Colleagues

When Mr. Ignatz leaves at 5:30 p.m., I gather my purse and notebooks and then leave for a drive to the Philadelphia suburbs, where I participate in an ongoing study group of child psychoanalysts. This group has been meeting for some forty years, and I have been a member since I moved to this area in 1995. At some point I became the unofficial "recorder," who summarizes the discussion and distributes minutes to group members, along with reading for the next month's meeting; now I am formally a co-chair of the group. I initially welcomed the opportunity to provide the minutes as a way to keep myself immersed in psychoanalytic thinking (despite occasional resentment at the work required). Since I am the only psychoanalyst in my area, I have few opportunities to think with others about the sorts of issues that psychoanalysts routinely consider, and I usually look forward to the discussions.

The ninety-minute drive is through beautiful countryside, on an interstate highway with limited access, but I have done it enough times that I seldom think about the scenery any more. On the drive tonight, I think about the case we are discussing in this month's group, one I wrote up years ago, during my psychoanalytic training: an adolescent girl who, during her analysis with me, became psychotic in the American sense (out of touch with reality).

I still remember the difficulties the girl and I lived through together in an analysis that was almost as difficult for me as for her. I remember vividly the feeling of helplessness as I saw her, day after day, sinking further into her regression, becoming more and more confused and disorganized, while I had no idea of how to stop the falling apart. My supervisor helped to "ground" me with discussions of theory and a reassurance that I was not making major mistakes; and the director of the inpatient hospital unit where she was eventually admitted also helped by taking responsibility for the day-to-day management (including medication) so I could stay in the noncontrolling role of the analyst. I will never forget my confusion and anxiety as the girl worsened day by day; and I will certainly never forget the day that I sat at her bedside in the general medical hospital, imagining that she was dying and it was my fault because I had misdiagnosed a medical problem as a hysterical conversion disorder.

Luckily for both of us, I had not in fact misdiagnosed the problem, and she began to improve the next day. Over the next two weeks she could be seen daily coming back to herself. The reading I have been doing about Winnicott seems particularly relevant to this young woman's treatment. I believed then, and still believe, that it was the "holding" and containment of the analytic process that allowed her first to regress so catastrophically, but then also allowed her to reintegrate herself in a fashion that apparently resolved many of the issues plaguing her life up until that point. She did pull herself back together, finding a new and less problem-ridden way to be herself in the face of the pressures in her life, and expressed her surprise and gratitude that I had been able to tolerate her "craziness" during that time.

I have always wondered if I might, with more experience, have been able to allow the regressive undoing of this girl's defenses to make room for a healthier personality structure without the falling apart that she experienced, and I hope that the group discussion will shed some light on this issue.

The group discussion is lively, interesting, and supportive of the nontraditional approach I was forced to take in dealing with this profoundly ill young woman. The members of the group also recognize how anxious I was at the time, as a young professional learning a new skill but forced to work outside the commonly accepted protocols of her new profession. They do not, however, offer any new insights into whether it might have been possible to have an equally good outcome without such a traumatic process.

As I drive home at the end of the evening, on city streets and local highways rather than the interstate (since I have no time pressure), I am tired, but feeling good about my professional self and my ability to help very ill people. Making my way home, I am acutely aware that my solid grounding in theory helped me to survive this crisis as well as the helpless, impotent feelings that came with it. I was able to still be available to my patient, even when she was suffering and I could not fix that. The theory reminded me that it was not my task to "fix" the crisis, or to give advice, but to understand the origins of the crisis and to help my patient figure out her own solutions. That allowed me then to keep going, even when I didn't understand what was happening, because I believed that there was meaning somewhere. With the theory to contain *me,* I could contain the overwhelming affect—the "craziness"—without abandoning the patient and without interrupting what she needed to do. Because I had my own "holding environment" (with my supervisor and in conversations with colleagues), I could allow my patient to be as crazy as she needed to be in order to find the meaning in her symptoms. I could allow it only because I knew there *was* meaning, and we were not hopeless.

Chapter 4

Wednesday

As I wait for Ms. Austin Wednesday morning, I hope she will bring up the issue of boundaries again, but I remind myself that I shouldn't have particular hopes or expectations about it. She does not return to that subject, but reports on a "real good day" at work, where she got some significant praise for her professional work. She says, "I really like that … probably too much," and adds, "I know I'm good at what I do, but I feel much better when I get praise," as if it were a bad thing.

I say, "It sounds like you're not supposed to be proud of yourself." She agrees, and adds that her parents always expected her to be the best at everything, but they didn't praise her when she was. They seemed to want the praise for themselves as good parents rather than allowing her to feel proud.

As I listen, mostly I notice that she is avoiding the very charged material about our relationship. Later, and as I write this, I know that she was not in fact avoiding that topic (or at least not only avoiding it): she was letting me know more about why she needed so badly to have proof that people love her, because she did not feel loved by her parents. On this Wednesday I do not comment on the avoidance, but try to stay with her as she talks about her current life stresses.

In our training, we learn to try not to dictate what our patients talk about in any given session. Bion (1967) tells us we should approach each session "without memory or desire," because if we try to "nudge" our patients to talk about what we want, often we miss what they need to talk about, and we may "nudge" them completely away from the important things that interfere with their way of being in the world. I cannot make myself not want Ms. Austin to return to the issue of our relationship, but I can at least not act on that want, and instead wait for her to do it in her own time.

Anne Alvarez describes the analyst's neutral stance as one of active noninterference, an "even-handed nonjudgmental interest in ... the inner lives and motives" of our patients, that neither steers away from nor repels any particular content or emotion. It is not a passive receptivity, but an active setting aside of our own wishes, emotions, or judgments in the service of allowing the patient to feel "recognized and known in all the sides of his nature" (Alvarez 1985). Borgogno and Fortune (2008) describe this active neutrality as "deferring to the preconscious and letting an answer emerge from it without immediately determining a response." I try to meet my patients at all times using this active neutrality (although of course sometimes, being human, I fail to achieve that goal). My hope is, and my experience tells me, that when I can maintain this active neutrality sufficiently, and can wait with patience and with the flexibility to allow them to control the progress of the treatment, my patients are usually able to find the elements in themselves that allow them to be grounded and emotionally whole.

Winnicott (again!) addresses this issue when he writes about the "non-impinging" or nonprescriptive analyst, who creates a space in which the patient can develop in his own way. The nonprescriptive analyst tries *not* to offer a path that her patient might follow at the cost of his authentic self (Winnicott 1960).

After Ms. Austin leaves, I leave the office for a house call, to see Ms. Quinn, a middle-aged woman with overwhelming anxiety and agoraphobia who is severely depressed. She has been unable to leave her house for the last two years because of the anxiety and depression; she came to my office for the first years of her treatment, but then as she got worse we began having telephone sessions. After about eighteen months of weekly telephone sessions, which did little more than help her to get by but not to improve, I decided that a "house call" would be appropriate, at least for a few weeks to months. I began seeing her weekly at her house about two months ago, going on a Wednesday because I try to keep that day fairly light (to allow myself time to write), so I have the time free to travel across town and back.

Over the years, I have made house calls only a few times: once for a child whose parents could not get her to come in for sessions (until she decided she didn't hate me after all), once for a patient dying of a physical illness who needed to speak with me but could not come in. I always feel as if I am doing something slightly wrong, because it is such a departure from what I usually do. It also is harder for me to stay focused on my patient and what she is saying when I am distracted by unfamiliar surroundings. I am aware of these issues with Ms. Quinn, but it does seem to be helpful to her so far, so I persist.

In the first of the "house calls," I began with Ms. Quinn as if I were meeting her for the first time: collecting a history and reviewing her history of medications as well as reviewing her decline since I first met her, hoping to understand what is happening now. She has sought second opinions with other professionals, but nobody has offered anything that we have not already tried; and no one offered ideas about why she appears to be getting worse and not better. After the re-evaluation in the first of the home visits, I began her on an older medication, not used much now because of side effects, and it seems to be making at least a slight difference. She is now able to get up, to shower and dress, and to do some of the housework that she has not done for more than a year; and she is feeling guardedly optimistic about what may come in the future. We plan that in our next visit I will drive her to the office for a session there; then we will have one or a few sessions where I come to the house and we drive in her car to the office. If all goes well with this slowly lessening dependence on me, she will again come to the office for her therapy.

This is certainly not traditional therapy; and in fact many psychiatrists would argue that it is counterproductive, that Ms. Quinn needs to be responsible for her own transportation, that to reach out to her in this way is enabling. I do worry about that and about this departure from the traditional frame of therapy. It seems fairly obvious to me, however, that medication has not provided a solution; and that if Ms. Quinn cannot get herself in to the office for therapy, no therapy will be taking place. I think it is both acceptable and helpful to reach out to her enough to at least make our interaction possible; I am somewhat comforted by remembering the supervisor during my training who told me to "do whatever it takes to keep the treatment alive, then figure out what it means." In going to Ms. Quinn's house, I am keeping the treatment alive, and later—when she is more functional—we can talk about what that meant to her.

I plan to do as little of the house calls—which may in fact encourage some dependence on me—as I can get away with, without discontinuing the therapy completely. My hope is that some temporary support through understanding how frightening it is for Ms. Quinn to leave the house, together with a different medication that seems to be reducing the intensity of the agoraphobia, will allow her to get back to a higher level of functioning, and we can return to the more traditional model of office-based therapy.

Importance of Frame

Many people have written about the importance of the frame, or setting, in analytic psychotherapy. Robert Langs (because he has strong views about the frame) and Donald Winnicott (because I've been reading a lot of his work lately) are the two that come first to my mind. If the office setting is the analyst's first clinical intervention, the establishment and maintenance of the frame are perhaps the most pervasive interventions. When we talk about the frame of therapy, we are referring to practical arrangements, including length of appointments, frequency and times of appointments, fees, and policies about cancellations, late sessions, or missed sessions. In specifically psychoanalytic psychotherapy, the term also refers to the "basic rule" of talking as freely as possible without censoring one's thoughts (free association), and policies about contact outside the analytic hour, including phone calls, emails, and social contact.

Langs and Winnicott take generally antithetical views. Langs (1981) suggests that the frame of psychotherapy must be relatively invariable, with few or no exceptions to one's usual practices. He believes that most changes in the frame, or exceptions to general policies, arise from transference and countertransference issues that are not being identified and discussed. Concerning sessions missed because of illness, for instance, he asserts that "Careful observation indicates that virtually every illness that occurs during therapy serves the total personality as a means of expressing unconscious fantasies related to unresolved intrapsychic conflicts and reflects resistances on some level. Therefore, illnesses are a nonverbal means of acting out; they interfere with verbalized insight and directly adaptive responses" (120). He does recommend some flexibility, and comments that "The underlying principles involve the need for the psychotherapist to be in reality a reasonably available, non-seductive, non-punitive, and not overly-demanding individual. This is important not only for the unfolding of the material necessary for successful treatment but also for the therapist to be a positive model of identification for the patient. In addition, the therapist's stance should be one that fosters trust and promotes a strong therapeutic alliance; if not, unanalyzable resistances and rage will undermine the therapy" (126).

In reading Langs's prolific writings, and in hearing him speak at times in the past, I have developed the impression that Langs believed that most parameters (deviations from the frame by the therapist) are mistakes arising from either ignorance or countertransference problems. He says (135) that "Repeated experience has taught me that patients in phases of resistance can very cleverly use and manipulate reality to provide themselves with seemingly unquestionable facades for acting out their resistances against treatment," and he appears to see most requests for deviations in the frame as acting out of resistances against treatment. An example of this sort of acting out (the term we use for "acting out" one's emotional responses instead of talking about them) would be the patient I described on Monday, who cancelled an appointment ostensibly for work reasons when he truly wanted to avoid talking about issues at hand.

Winnicott takes a very different approach, starting (1989a) with the belief that for psychoanalysis to be successful the analyst must adapt to the patient's needs. He tells us (1960) that emotional development, whether in early life or in therapy, is a process of maturation, with growth based on the accumulation of experiences. When a child has not had the experiences needed for the various steps of development, therapy can sometimes offer them in the context of the therapeutic relationship. Winnicott's view of psychoanalysis is clearly one in which the process of therapy parallels the processes of healthy development, and the hope is to allow healthy development to resume through the treatment. Winnicott apparently would agree with the supervisor who advocated doing "whatever is needed to keep the treatment alive, and analyze it later."

Meeting the patient's needs does not mean that we must do whatever the patient asks. It does, however, mean that for some patients, using parameters—exceptions to the generally established frame of the therapy—is acceptable and indeed crucial (Winnicott 1989a). Winnicott believes that for patients who have had significant failures of environmental provision early in life—practically speaking, those who today we would see as having character or personality disorders—"the provision and maintenance of the setting are more important than the interpretive work" (ibid, 96).

However, he goes on to say, in an ongoing therapy the patient may begin to make demands on the analyst for particular sorts of behavior, and the analyst must comply so as not to disrupt the therapeutic alliance: "It is as if the patient gradually seduces us into collusion, collusion with the infant in the patient who in some way or other received inadequate attention at the earliest stages" (ibid, 97). He offers the example of a patient for whom the curtains in the room, arrangement of the furniture, and objects on the desk all had to be present and in exactly the right position. When he failed one day to achieve this (having moved one of the objects on his desk), she was devastated, and it took most of the hour for her to be calm enough to talk about her reaction to the "mistake." The incident was ultimately helpful, in that Winnicott and the patient were able eventually (once the patient was calm again) to identify elements in her history that had led her to be so intolerant of change.

Winnicott sees this demandingness as arising from regression in the treatment as the patient "gradually begins to get hope that [his] demands will be met. It is only because of the development in the patient that there is this gradual increase of the need for a specialised environmental provision. In the kind of case I am talking about it is never a question of giving satisfactions in the ordinary manner of succumbing to a seduction. It is always that if one provides certain conditions work can be done and if one does not provide these conditions work cannot be done and one might as well not try. The patient is not there to work with us except when we provide the conditions which are necessary" (ibid, 97).

He goes on to say that "gradually if one attempts to meet the patient's needs of the kind I am describing, the demands made on the analyst become very great," (ibid, 98), and "it may easily be that one can carry two or perhaps even three cases but not four at the same time" (ibid, 100).

Langs and Winnicott clearly have different views about the issue of maintaining the frame, but there is some overlap; and thinking about each of them, comparing and contrasting their ideas, gives me ways of thinking productively about Ms. Quinn. I once heard it said (although I don't remember by whom) that the more theories you know, the more ways you have to think about your patients; and I do find this to be true. Theories do not accompany us into the hour with our patient, but they provide a background for thinking in the hour about what the patient is communicating and experiencing.

Patients Who Refuse Treatment Recommendations

After meeting with Ms. Quinn, I run a few errands, have lunch, and then return to the office. Although I usually try not to schedule appointments on Wednesdays except for Ms. Austin and Ms. Quinn and keep the time for reading and writing, in this particular week I am more than usually busy (because of the vacation), and have had to take some of my "protected" day to see patients who could not come on other days.

I meet with Mr. Robinson, an older man who came into treatment when he was first depressed and has continued as he has developed more serious symptoms of a psychotic process with paranoid thinking (he believes his ex-employer is managing the traffic lights in the town so he must sit at a red light for much longer than usual). He has refused any medication for either depression or psychosis, but finds the therapy sessions very helpful in managing the anxiety that I believe underlies his paranoia. He talks about his job loss, his inability to work now, and the stresses in his life, while I listen and look for ways to help him acknowledge that his suspicion of others is not realistic, as well as to persuade him to try taking some medication that might reduce his paranoid thinking.

> I usually have a fairly high level of therapeutic optimism—
> the belief that given time my patient and I can find a way to
> help relieve their suffering—but it is quite difficult with Mr.
> Robinson. He clearly values his time with me, and will say that
> my listening to him is the only thing that keeps him going;
> but he consistently refuses the medication, which I believe is
> the only thing that can help quickly with the paranoia and
> distorted thinking. He is not dangerous to himself or to others,
> so I cannot have him hospitalized against his will; and if I try to
> suggest hospitalization, he believes for at least a few moments
> that I am also against him, that I have "joined up with Them."
> I have stopped suggesting hospitalization in order to preserve
> our therapeutic alliance, and to maintain some possibility of
> eventually persuading him to take antipsychotic medication, but
> at times I dread seeing him because it reminds me of how helpless

I am to be more immediately effective. As with some other patients, I struggle to listen for unconscious communications, to remain the "nonintrusive therapist," and to find ways to make those unconscious communications conscious, without simply stepping back and becoming a passive, noninteractive listener.

Disruption and Repair in the Therapeutic Alliance

With Mr. Robinson, as with other similar patients, it is crucial to tend to the therapeutic alliance because of his high level of paranoia and suspicion. If he believes that I have "joined up with Them," that I do not have his best interest in mind, he will bolt from the therapy, and will most likely not be willing to see anyone else. Mr. Robinson requires more flexibility than most of my patients to maintain the therapeutic alliance and keep him working with me. Psychoanalysts know, though, that part of what allows for growth is the cycle of disruption and repair: each time Mr. Robinson feels I have failed to understand, or that I am not listening, or that I have turned against him, our relationship is disrupted. When I am able to convey that I do in fact understand, or I am able to listen more accurately and show him that I have listened, or I am able to establish that I am still "on his side" even when we disagree, we strengthen very slightly his ability to tolerate having others disagree without feeling attacked.

This pattern of disruption and repair is present in all therapies, although it often takes place under the surface and is not problematic enough to require conscious attention from therapist or patient. It is similar to the way in which young children learn to tolerate frustration: being told no by mother and father, where there is affection coexisting with the frustration, makes it possible for the child to learn to tolerate frustration without letting her anger destroy the relationship completely. That is how we begin to learn anger management, and to be able to be angry with people we love without leaving them or hurting them. Mr. Robinson's early life did not make it possible for him to achieve that particular piece of emotional development, and he is still struggling with knowing how to manage in a world that is entirely frustrating to him.

Today Mr. Robinson tells me that he is getting a puppy to raise. He clearly is excited and pleased, and I suspect that he wants a dog because he has no one else in his life who can love him as unconditionally as a dog can and will. As is almost always the case, he wants me to agree with everything he says, and if I simply listen without agreeing or disagreeing, he is disappointed; but he is able to allow me to comment on his wish to be loved by the dog because he feels no one else does, without feeling insulted or criticized. He rushes out of the office in the hurry that he always feels, needing to be on the move so as not to have to stop and feel how empty his life has become with the loss of all his close relationships to his paranoia.

After Mr. Robinson, I have an appointment with Ms. Soames, but she does not show up for it. While I am waiting for her, I find that Janet is free, and I stop in her office to talk informally. We have both had very difficult, emotionally powerful sessions in the last several days, and she has asked to be able to "dump the affect": to talk with me about her own feelings in the charged sessions, to assist her to gain some perspective and be less overwhelmed by the intensity of the sessions. The opportunity to do this is one of the benefits of working in a group rather than alone;

and Janet, Heidi, and I all do some of this "offloading" of the emotions we absorb during painful sessions. I say a little about Mr. Robinson, and how difficult it is for me to listen patiently and not get angry when he again refuses even to consider medication that might help him to function, but how important I know it is to allow him to remain in control of his own life. We also talk about the pain and frustration Janet feels at listening to a woman with PTSD who is being traumatized again by an uncaring, judgmental, and highly stressful work situation. We both agree that until the woman is willing to leave her job, she is likely to make little progress toward feeling better. Like me with Mr. Robinson, Janet is feeling helpless and impotent to find effective interventions for this woman who is suffering greatly. Also like me with Mr. Robinson, she knows that staying with the process, and continuing to listen and trying to understand, is the best hope in the long run for positive change.

Ms. Soames does not show for her appointment. I will not call her—I tend not to want to "chase after" patients, and to allow them to decide what they can or cannot do in their treatment—but I make a note to myself to be sure to ask about the missed appointment when and if I do see her again, and to be aware of how long it takes her to call for another appointment.

Free Association

My next appointment is with Tom, an eight-year-old boy who was brought by his parents for "counseling or psychotherapy" because of a change in his behavior patterns in recent months: he has not been particularly bad, but is acting out in small ways, not doing his homework as promptly as he used to, not always doing what he is told, often arguing back. The parents both have experienced the value of psychotherapy and are hoping their son will be able to benefit from talking with me. Tom is, like many boys, not used to talking much about his feelings, and often struggles to find things to say at the beginning of the hour. He does usually find it fairly easy to talk freely once we get started, so we have fallen into a habit of his reporting on events of the week as a way to help him get started.

Today, Tom talks about playing football at school, and how someone sprained an ankle; then he tells me that he and his father went fly-fishing, and they nearly hooked someone with their line as they were casting. He goes on to describe playing with a remote-control airplane, which they nearly ran into someone; and then he complains that when he wanted to skateboard, his mother made him wear elbow pads and kneepads.

I listen to Tom for about fifteen minutes, and then I say, "You know, you've told me three or four stories about people getting hurt. Are you maybe worried about something like that?" He thinks for a minute, and then says, "Yeah! How did you know that?" He goes on to say that he had been in a minor motor vehicle accident earlier in the week. He was not hurt himself, but since then he has been a little anxious about things that might go wrong. He did not consciously recognize that he was worrying about people getting hurt, but his unconscious mind "selected out" things for him to talk about that showed the pattern in his thoughts.

This is how free association works: the basic rule is that if people come in and say, as best they can, whatever is in their mind, patterns will emerge that allow us to know more about what is going on in the back of their minds. My expertise is to listen and find those patterns and the recurring themes that will allow me to understand my patients' behaviors and their psychological symptoms.

After Tom, I make two last phone calls, and then I go home relatively early, planning to do some reading and to work on a paper I am writing at home.

Chapter 5

Thursday

In today's 8:00 a.m. appointment, the last for the week with Ms. Austin, I again wonder if she will bring up the issue of boundaries.

She begins by talking about business issues, focusing on an incident at work in which she feels she should warn a colleague that he is being "too nice" to her, and that he needs to look out for himself more.

> I don't think of it at the time, but later I wonder if she was warning me to look out for myself with her.

After a few moments, she says, "We talked yesterday about our relationship ..." I said, "In fact it was the day before. I was waiting to see if you would bring it up again."

"That troubles me ... why wouldn't you ask?"

"Waiting lets me have some idea about how hard it is for you to bring it up. Plus, I wanted to give you the space to not talk about it until you're ready."

She says again that the idea of the analyst being changed by the analysis is new to her, that she has been thinking of our relationship as "a more traditional doctor-patient relationship" where the doctor acts *on* the patient, not *with* the patient. She understands the idea, and it rings true for her, but then she applies it to our relationship: "I don't get to see what you are going through, or understand what the analysis means to you. Wouldn't that be useful?" (said in a wistful tone).

I ask, "Useful ... to me or to you?"

"To me."

"Can you tell me how knowing that might be useful to you?"

Her thoughtful response is, "How do I know what's for me and what's for you?"

After a few moments, when it is clear she has nothing more to say, I say, "That's what I meant the other day about the rules being for me, not for you. The way it *should* work is that you can talk about sexual feelings, you can be angry at me, you can express being attracted to me, you can even ask for a sexual liaison with me; I'm supposed to listen without criticism or shock, I won't refuse to talk about it, but I should absolutely not ever *act* in any way that suggests that your wish—to know more about me, to be close to me— can be fulfilled. Knowing that nothing will happen about the wish is what makes the 'forbidden wish' safe to talk about, and lets you understand how that wish may play itself out in other relationships and at other times. If Dr. Z had done that, it could have helped you to understand your relationship with Joe [the high school teacher] and why you couldn't get away from him. You could have worked it out and maybe avoided some of the problems you had in later relationships with other men."

Again, Ms. Austin thinks about what I have said; after several minutes, she asks, "How does that translate to you?"

"With me, it has a lot to do with all the stuff about wanting people—wanting me—to like you, and taking care of me so I will. And with wanting a friendship with me."

"Talking about it would feel like I was nagging, or trying to trick you."

"That's called working through …"

"It feels like I'm trying to get you to change your mind."

"And that's not okay?"

"I should play by the rules."

"Again, the rules are for me, not for you."

She thinks it seems unfair, that all the burden of maintaining the boundaries should be on me; I agree that sometimes it's hard for me, but I agreed to it because it is a part of my job, and those boundaries make it possible for us both to do the work of her analysis.

After another moment, Ms. Austin asks if I have someone to whom I talk about my patients. I suspect she wants to know that I have some help with the feelings, that she wants to take care of me. I say that I do have someone to talk to (as I do in fact talk with colleagues), and immediately she says, "What do you say about me?"

With that question, I know that she's not thinking about taking care of me, but is worrying that I might be upset with her in some way, or criticize her; or perhaps she is hoping to hear about my positive feelings for her. I'm reminded of Winnicott's ideas about the importance of not knowing—allowing oneself to be uncertain about what a particular remark means until the patient lets us know. Avoiding this sort of premature uncertainty is important because we might be wrong, as I was here. It's also important, though, for the patient to have the experience herself of finding meaning in her thoughts, instead of having it "given" to her by an interpretation.

This exchange is at the very end of the hour and of her week; I say, "For that question, we need to understand what it means to you before I decide whether to answer it. But for today we have to stop." She laughs, saying "That's convenient!" and with a smile I respond, "Also, it gives me time to figure out how to answer you!"

As she stands up off the couch, I hand her an invoice, as I do at the end of each week. Today she asks if I included charges for the previous week, when she unexpectedly missed the last day and didn't get that week's invoice. I say yes, and add, "You really are taking care of me, even about money!" She laughs again, and then leaves the room for the front desk, where I take a payment by credit card and say good-bye to her.

After she leaves, as I'm walking back down the hall to my office I think about how Ms. Austin's analysis has in fact affected me. She uses intellectualization and thinking *about* things instead of feeling them as a way to manage her emotions; because I also intellectualize at times, it's very easy for me to lapse into teaching and explaining things, as I did in these sessions. For me, that sort of explaining in everyday language is helpful because it reminds me of the power of what I do and why I do it. This in turn helps me to have more "faith" in the process itself, and to be more confident in myself and about the work. Today, though, I remember that I need to be particularly alert not to let either Ms. Austin or myself—or both of us—lapse into thinking about her *only* intellectually: if we lose sight of the emotion that drives her behavior, the analysis will stall.

Supervision

After getting another cup of coffee, I go to my desk and sign online for a supervisory session with Xiao, one of the people who are learning psychoanalytic psychotherapy through the China American Psychoanalytic Alliance. In addition to the individual therapy with Ms. Ma, who met with me on Tuesday, I supervise two individual psychotherapists weekly, and for three months in the winter I teach a clinical case conference. In the individual supervision, I meet weekly with the therapists and they bring process notes (written notes as close to verbatim reports of their sessions with their patients as they can manage). We talk about how to understand the material, how they responded to what their patients said, what other possible responses might be, what the patient's reaction was to their comments, what the therapist's reaction to the patient was, and what the underlying meaning of the interactions with the patient might be. In many ways, the supervisory experience is the most important part of one's training in psychoanalysis and psychotherapy. Theory and technique are useful and important, but until you know what to do in the room with the patient, and have some experience in applying theory to the actual interactions with the patient, you cannot know what therapy is like.

For me, supervising and teaching are also important. I believe that beyond a certain level of experience, the best way to keep learning is to teach others. With everyone I teach, I learn something about my work, or I am reminded of something I once knew but have forgotten. When students ask you why you do something in a particular way, sometimes you have to admit that it is a bad habit, and the honest teacher will change her habits. Or you discover that you have drifted into doing something without noticing, for good reasons that you can then pass on to others. I also find—as with Ms. Austin—that when I have to figure out how to say something in "regular English," not using jargon, I understand it better myself; and over the years I

121

have decided that when I cannot explain it in "regular English," most likely I don't really understand it at all.

Teaching, with people who are just beginning their careers, also reminds me of how difficult this work can be. I am so used to it that sometimes it feels easy; but in fact it requires constant monitoring for sloppiness, so I go to conferences, and I talk with colleagues about my work. Today, I'm supervising Major—the English nickname for Xiao (since mostly Americans are unable to pronounce Chinese names correctly). He talks about his recent beginning at a local clinic, where he sees people hour after hour with few breaks and with little time to complete the copious paperwork that is required. I remember vividly the days when I was not in control of my own schedule and had to do the same thing.

Moving from Patient to Patient

Major is talking about how upset he was earlier in the week when one of his clinic patients was talking about suicidal ideas; he thinks he was able to help her, but now worries that he did not do enough.

My patients sometimes will ask how I can do my work, how I can listen to everyone and not be overwhelmed by the pain and the distress. In my early years, I had to learn to move from one patient to the next, quickly immersing myself in the internal world of someone who might be enormously different from the last patient I had listened to, because I didn't have time to make the shift anything but quickly.

122

One of the skills I learned was to compartmentalize what I know about each person I work with. These days I find that I don't really remember the details of any given patient's history or treatment unless I am in the room with her, or unless I have been discussing his treatment with a colleague for several minutes. I have learned a sort of state-dependent memory which lets me enter into the psychic space that belongs to the patient I am focused on. I drop into the psychic space that lets me feel and think with my patient, instead of being in the space in my head that "belongs" to me. With the next patient, then, I shift from the psychic space of the first to that of the next, with a different set of emotions, associations, and connectedness, but I inhabit that second space as fully as I inhabited the first, or as I inhabit my own psychic space.

One of the consequences of this state-dependent memory is that I seldom am plagued by memories of the pains and griefs of my patients unless I am deliberately focusing on their history and their lives. This allows me to be available to others without interference, and it also allows me to fully experience the griefs and joys of my own life without interference by the griefs and joys of others. On the rare occasion when I do find myself preoccupied with what I have heard in my office, I know that it has touched one of my own charged issues, and that I must be particularly careful about the countertransference responses with that patient. (Countertransference is the therapist's emotional reaction to the patient, the counterpoint to the transference, which is the patient's emotional reaction to the therapist.) Each set of emotional reactions has links to the history and past relationships of that individual; so when I experience particularly strong countertransference reactions to a patient, I know that my own history and my own individual quirks have been stirred up.

By now, it is second nature to me to take the step that moves my attention from one patient to the next, to inhabit what I have called that person's psychic space. I am able automatically to fall into the reverie (described on Tuesday) that allows me to listen for patterns, to listen below the surface meaning of the conversation, but not to lose track of the surface itself. In the words of Janna Malamud Smith (2012, 19), "The focus with which I listen to patients often switches itself on reflexively when someone ... speaks frankly. The habit of listening so particularly is engrained after decades." Occasionally it surprises me how effortless it seems, and how little I have to work to be immersed in the internal world of another.

In my early years, as I learned to shift my focus from myself or from one patient to the patient in the room with me, I also planted deeply the awareness that it is not my job to "fix" things for my patients, or to tell them how to live their lives. It is my job to help them understand themselves, and to recognize how they contribute to the crises in their lives, so that they can find ways of managing themselves and their lives independently. This awareness also helps me to let go and to not be plagued in my nonworking hours by the struggles of my patients. I wonder sometimes how I can care so deeply within the hour, but then let go as they leave, even as I know that I could not continue to do the work if I could not both care deeply and let go.

I do have days when I find myself on the verge of losing the capacity to shift focus, of shutting off the reverie: at these times, I have too much unprocessed affect floating around in my mind because I have had several difficult sessions with no time to let things "settle." Generally, if I can take fifteen minutes to just do nothing, or to read something nonprofessional, I can find my balance and go back to allowing my mind to float freely, to access my capacity for reverie. With that capacity restored, I am once again able to let myself make the unconscious and near-unconscious connections that in turn help patients recognize previously unknown aspects of themselves.

In supervision, as with Major, I am trying to help my supervisees master this way of letting one's mind roam freely, and to help them learn the reflexive shift of focus that moves us through the day from one patient to the next.

After the online session with Major, I have several medication management appointments in a row, as had been the case on Monday. Two of the three are doing reasonably well and are ready to return to their primary care physicians (family doctor, internist, or pediatrician) for medication monitoring, since their prescription regimen is fairly simple, they are stable, and we expect that they will continue to do well.

When Patients Don't Do Well

The third is Ms. Upjohn, a young woman with significant depression and anxiety who has been in treatment with me for several years. Initially her depression appeared to be fairly simple, likely to respond to medication. However, over the years we have tried all of the current, commonly used antidepressants and any other medication I could think of that might make some difference for her. She cannot tolerate most of the medications because of side effects; of the ones she can tolerate, none are particularly helpful. She has also made several attempts at engaging

125

in psychotherapy, with both Janet and Heidi and with me, but has not found it useful. Finally she stopped all attempts at psychotherapy.

I have not refused to see her, despite her not being in therapy, because she does have a solid working relationship with me about medication. If I did refuse, she would probably go to another physician for her medication, and that doctor would also try all the possible physical interventions available, with the accompanying side effects and medical risks, and she would again not benefit. Ms. Upjohn and I have found a combination of medications that allows her to continue on a daily basis without feeling suicidal or completely despairing, and she will talk with me briefly about her life stresses during her medication checks. Her life is not what either of us would hope for: she still has consistent and overwhelming anxiety with occasional panic attacks, and finds little or nothing in her life enjoyable. Today we review her medications, confirm that there are no new medications that are likely to be helpful to her, and talk briefly about the stresses in her life. Every few months—but not today—she will say something in this part of the interview that lets us look at some of what is under the surface of her chronic and debilitating anxiety and depression. Today, after talking about the last month's events, we make another appointment for the next month, and she leaves, leaving me to feel helpless, stuck, and incapable for a few moments, until I must move on to the next thing in my day.

I suspect that every physician has a few patients like Ms. Upjohn, where medication has failed to help. I know that most therapists have had the experience of feeling that nothing we can do helps, and we feel stuck and incapable. In those situations, we have to decide whether to just give up and stop trying or to stay engaged with the patient, hoping that some day we will find a way to help. In my own case, I almost always stay with the patient, looking for new possibilities. I may encourage them to look for a second opinion, in hopes that another physician can do what I have been unable to do (and I may hope that they do go elsewhere for care). But I am unwilling to send them away as long as they want to keep trying with me.

As the next thing I must do, I deal with a few phone calls about refills and a call from Ms. Soames, who had missed her appointment on Wednesday. She calls to say very apologetically that she had completely forgotten the appointment, and we reschedule. This is an ongoing concern for her: she has ADHD, which is very disorganizing for her, as well as anxiety that makes it hard for her to hold on to her lists and the ways she tries to stay organized. She is quite relieved that I am not angry and that I am willing to reschedule.

Langs would say that I should not reschedule but charge for the missed appointment and simply expect Ms. Soames to keep her next standing appointment. I choose not to do that because it does not fit my style of functioning and does not feel right to me; but I will explore with her the unconscious meaning of her absence. I also will review with her what she is doing about her ADHD and what she is doing to improve her general level of organization.

At this time in my practice, Thursdays are usually my most difficult day: not because what I am doing is more difficult than other days, but because usually I have very few breaks. Today is very different, and this slower-paced morning feels like a break since everything is going smoothly. I greet my 11:00 a.m. patient with a sense that this is a good day (aside from Ms. Upjohn), likely to feel easy and not particularly stressful.

At 11:00 I see Vance, a student at a local college. He came to me because he disliked the health center at his college but needs medication and psychotherapy for his significant depression. He has finished the semester and is leaving for the summer; he plans to meet regularly with the therapist he had in his home community and then return to see me when he returns for school in the fall. We talk briefly about how he can protect himself from "triggering" problems if he runs into his ex-girlfriend (because the relationship with her has been a major issue for him), and make sure that he can contact me if he needs over the summer. I offer the possibility of online sessions to help maintain the relationship, and wish him an enjoyable summer. I don't expect to hear from him over the summer because he has a therapist in his hometown who is a significant support for him. I believe that he has as-yet unrecognized concerns about whether people in his life will abandon him, and I believe it is important to facilitate a continuing relationship with his therapist at home while at the same time making it clear that I continue to be available.

Rewards of the Work

At noon, I have thirty minutes for lunch, and then I meet with Wendy, a young woman who is just getting ready to go off to college. I saw her first when she was about ten, for significant depression. We met weekly then for about a year, with a very positive response, and she returned at about thirteen for what she called "a tune up," with a brief recurrence of her depression. I saw her another two or three times in the intervening years, each time only for one or two sessions, to remind us both of what we had learned and how she had grown. When she called for today's appointment, I wondered if she was having difficulties with depression related to anxiety about leaving home; but in fact she says she wants to thank me for having been a part of her growing up. She is now a very impressive, quite mature young woman who I believe will do quite well, and I am moved and pleased to have been able to be helpful to her. We don't often get this sort of recognition from our patients: it is considered an excellent outcome if they just go on with their lives and don't ever have to think about us again. But when people do take the time for this sort of thank you, it is always moving and gratifying.

Occasionally I am asked about what I enjoy about my work, and I find it a hard question to answer. I am quite clear that what I do is energizing and lively, and that I would not want to do anything else with my life. But then my "professional" voice says to me, "Wait a minute. You're supposed to approach your patients without memory or desire ... so how does that fit?"

Of course we do have wishes and desires about our work, like anybody does. We want to make enough money to live on; we want to feel like we are doing something worthwhile; we want to believe that we are making a difference in the world. The question of what are gratifications are "legitimate" and what are "illegitimate" has been discussed at length in the analytic literature because we all hear stories about sexual seduction of patients, or therapists using the patient to meet their narcissistic needs at the patient's expense. The emphasis on self-awareness for the therapist is intended to help make sure that our own emotional needs don't interfere with our ability to meet the needs of our patients.

But as Bacal and Thomson (1998, 249-170) tell us, "We believe that analysts regularly expect patients to respond in a number of ways that are, in fact, self-sustaining or self-enhancing. And our patients ongoingly meet a number of psychological needs that enable us to go on treating them. For the most part, we are unaware that this is happening." Mitchell (1997, 35) says that "not only is psychoanalysis a powerful, transformative experience for the patient, it also provides an extraordinary experience for the analyst. It is only in recent years, with the increasing openness in writing about countertransference, that it has been possible to acknowledge how absorbing, personally touching, and potentially transformative the practice of psychoanalysis can often be for the analyst."

Most therapists do find the work absorbing and fulfilling, but we need to remember that our patients do not owe us anything except payment of their bill. We may or may not receive gratitude, or admiration, or appreciation for our efforts; and in fact if these emotions are predominant, we have some obligation to interpret the idealizing transference (that is, to identify it as out of proportion to reality) and thereby reduce its intensity lest the patient start to feel she cannot do without us.

But we also need to acknowledge to ourselves that we do this work because we want to get something out of it more than a paycheck. If you are bright enough to be a good therapist, there are many easier ways to earn a paycheck—and most likely to earn more money than most therapists make! It is when we don't acknowledge that our work meets emotional needs for us that we slip into boundary violations, such as telling our personal problems to patients, making business deals or taking insider stock tips from them, having extra-analytic contact with them, having sexual relationships with them. On a smaller scale, if we are not aware of our own needs, we may "get something" from our patients by failing to notice attempts to end the therapy, being chronically late for sessions, taking nonemergency phone calls during sessions. Maroda suggests (2005) that if these smaller violations of the frame occur repeatedly and chronically, we should ask how and why this particular analyst feels personally or professionally frustrated in relation to this particular patient at this time, or if he has unresolved issues motivating him to seek power and personal convenience at his patients' expense. Constant monitoring of the frame, and of our maintenance of the frame, is the best way to avoid getting into trouble with boundary violations.

Frustrations of the Work

Today, the conversation with Wendy is pleasant and positive, in contrast to my next appointment, with Ms. Xerxes. Ms. Xerxes is one of the patients who reminds me that I need to be flexible and able to tolerate frustration and disappointment in order to continue the work. She is also a young adult whom I first saw as a child, when she was about eight years old, until her family took her elsewhere for treatment after a few months. She returned to therapy with me when she was in her junior year in high school, and has continued in treatment more or less continuously (with occasional interruptions for a few months) since. She now is in her twenties, has graduated from college, and is working in another city. She struggles enormously with regulating her emotions, with maintaining intimate relationships, and with being able to manage the stresses of everyday life. We meet online because she did not want to try to establish a therapeutic relationship with another therapist after she moved.

> For individuals with borderline personality disorder, like Ms. Xerxes, or for anyone who has trouble sustaining close relationships and with trusting others, a loss of a therapist can be devastating, making it impossible for them to find a new therapist. Although I prefer not to do long-distance therapy, I will do so for individuals who have seen me face-to-face for at least a year but who leave the area. In my mind, the main difficulty with internet psychotherapy is establishing the working relationship, and learning to "read" the emotional reactions of the other. We have established that relationship in the face-to-face work, and we know each other well enough to be able to read those cues. As I commented about Mr. Julian, however, the nature of the relationship changes when we are not face-to-face. Even with a history of a well-established relationship, I sometimes have trouble sustaining the feeling of connection in internet therapy, but it seems better than allowing the therapeutic process to be lost completely.

Today Ms. Xerxes is relatively positive and says her life is going well. I get nervous at times like this because my experience with Ms. Xerxes is that when she is feeling positive it usually ends precipitously. Even a slight reference to past difficulties can be felt by her as very critical and attacking, as if I am suggesting that she is "too crazy" to ever be well and that I *want* her to feel bad. I have to be very careful about making remarks designed to help her explore what accounts for her current good feelings or to help her begin to recognize what she can do to retain or regain those good feelings later. Sometimes I am tempted to reassure her about herself, but then I remember what Casement tells us (1991, 76), that "some countertransference is always operating when I deflect a patient, or try to reassure, particularly as I know so well that this does not work." When I try to reassure Ms. Xerxes, almost always she reacts as if I am denying her experience, not listening and not allowing her to feel her own feelings. I usually feel like I am walking a tightrope, where the best I can do is to stand still and not fall off, hoping all along to be able at some point to take a small step forward and eventually make it off the tightrope. Today we do not fall off, and Ms. Xerxes is still feeling positive and hopeful as we say good-bye.

Marital Therapy in Pieces

After Ms. Xerxes, I see Mr. Young, the husband in a couple to whom I am offering what I think of as marital therapy in pieces. I see each person in the couple individually, with the agreement that I can tell each anything I feel appropriate about what the other has said or done. They are having significant problems in their marriage, in part because of Mr. Young's recent, compulsively driven "confession" of years of having thought about other women; both spouses see this as infidelity, even though he never acted on the thoughts. Mrs. Young is struggling to find a way to forgive Mr. Young and go on with the marriage, despite feeling that she "must not have been enough for him." As Mr. Young tries to sort out why he can't be satisfied with his marriage, Mrs. Young is beginning to recognize that Mr. Young's thoughts are about *his* internal world, not about who *she* truly is. We stumbled across the analogy of gluten intolerance: if an individual cannot eat white bread, it's not the fault of the bread for containing gluten; the problem is within the individual eating the bread. In the same way, if Mr. Young finds a need to look at other women, the fault is not in Mrs. Young for being inadequate; it is in Mr. Young for not allowing himself to be satisfied.

I often feel that I am just feeling my way with the Youngs, and initially I was reluctant to take on this task. When Mr. Young's "confession" (apparently precipitated by a medical crisis) upset the family balance, however, they would not see anyone else. Some years before I had worked with their adopted child, helping with her very difficult transition to their home; and Mr. Young trusted me as he could not have trusted anyone else. The working-out of the process has proven to be very helpful to the Youngs, and I feel I have learned a great deal from working with them—learning things that will help me with others in the future. Today Mr. Young is newly aware of how his marital problems feel like some events from his early years, with parents who were never enough. We spend the hour trying to get clearer about how that might contribute to his present situation.

Play Therapy

After Mr. Young leaves, I check quickly to make sure the play area in my office (the dollhouse and the cabinets with toys) are in reasonable shape, and then I greet Zachary, an eight-year-old boy with great anxiety and problems in school. I don't see many children these days, I suspect because most people think of psychiatrists as doing only medication, and they are reluctant to medicate young children. This young man came to me because his family and teachers thought he had attention deficit hyperactivity disorder, and they all wanted ADHD medication (stimulants such as Ritalin or Dexedrine). When I saw Zach, I thought he had perhaps slight ADHD but a significant level of anxiety and an associated depression. Depression and anxiety can interfere significantly with concentration and focus in school; and anxiety in particular can lead children to be very "hyper" as they try to keep busy so as not to think about their fears. With Zach, I learned fairly quickly that when he came in wanting to do cartwheels in my office, something had happened to upset him during the week; and if we could find a way to talk about the upsetting incident, the cartwheels went away. Today, Zach is not particularly hyper, and wants to play *Chutes and Ladders*. He enjoys the simple game, and particularly enjoys my exaggerated exclamations of dismay when I hit a slide and must slide down the game board to be behind him. *Chutes and Ladders* is particularly useful in helping children learn to tolerate the frustrations of everyday life, as a frustration is so easily reversed if one lands on a ladder and is so clearly experienced when one has done nothing wrong but land on a slide.

With all of our patients, we try to attend to the unconscious communication that can be seen in body language, dress, sequence of thoughts, and so forth. With children, not uncommonly, they have no way to talk about their feelings in words, and so sometimes all we have is the unconscious communication. As I play with Zach, I am reminded of other children:

- a boy who played chess by putting his king in the corner, surrounded by all his men, so that he was completely safe but also could not move himself. This was exactly how he lived his life, safe from harm by others but unable to move or do anything constructive himself.
- a very young boy who played marbles, making up rules that allowed him to take all my marbles. At the end, as he picked up my last marble he announced, "Oh, I forgot! The person

that loses all their marbles first, wins!" He had great problems with aggression, but was nevertheless loving at times; and he had found a way to be aggressive (by taking the marbles) but also to save me from his aggression by the rules change.

Today, Zach laughs at me and enjoys my dismay when I lose to him three times in a row; he is, I believe, learning that it is possible for people to be aggressive without being hurtful (as when he wins the game but doesn't gloat), and to be "aggressed against" (as when he beats me in various games) without retaliating.

As Donald Winnicott says, when you can "reach your own aggression ... [and find] ... that the world in fact survives," then you can take "a look at your aggressiveness [and find] that it provides one of the roots of living energy." (Rodman, 1987, 184).

Returning Patients

At 5:00 p.m., I see Mr. Ignatz for his last session of the week. He comes only three days a week, a compromise we arrived at early in his treatment between his inability to pay anything close to a full fee and our mutual wish for a psychoanalysis to be possible for him. Today he begins the hour by paying his fee for the week in cash; he pays in cash because early in his treatment several of his checks bounced. He has expressed his belief that being required to pay in cash, rather than continuing to bounce checks, functioned as a "push" toward behaving as a responsible adult, and has said that he appreciated my ability to see him as at least potentially a responsible adult, even when he did not feel like one.

He is again silent for most of the hour. This time, however, he talks about a problem at work, when he was not able to solve a problem that was posed him; and he remembers, in that context, visiting a Montessori class prior to starting kindergarten.

This new memory suggests that the interchange on Tuesday, about the importance of a relationship where someone can reliably understand his needs without making demands, was on target because it has opened up new material in the form of a new memory.

He has a very vivid memory of seeing a huge bin full of numbered blocks and understanding that he was "supposed" to put the blocks in order. He could do that—but he also knew that he would never have enough time to finish because his family was going to be there only a few minutes, and there were hundreds of blocks. His terror of not being able to finish something that he is "supposed" to do has stayed with him for most of his life, and it may explain some of why he struggled so much in his school years.

In school, especially elementary school, as soon as a child accomplishes one task, he is praised and then given another task to finish. This is how we motivate children to continue learning; and for many (if not most) children, it works well. They respond to the praise by entering into the new task with confidence that they will be able to complete it. For Mr. Ignatz, however, it seems to have resulted in a sort of paralysis, with him being so afraid of not ever doing enough that he could not even begin a task. As I think about this, I wonder if that is a part of why he has spent so many hours in silence without leaving the analysis, even after we talked about that as a possibility: perhaps he is afraid he cannot do "enough" in the analysis and so cannot leave.

At the end of the hour Mr. Ignatz gets up and leaves without saying anything, as is his usual habit.

At the end of Thursday, I see Kyle for his second session of the week. He is again depressed and pessimistic, but today is more willing to talk about it: about how he feels isolated and alone, that his friends are not truly friends because they spend time with their girlfriends instead of him. He is increasingly sharing with me—in small bits scattered through the sessions—information about being intensely anxious, about social interactions, and about his ability to succeed in the world. Although he hides it well because he desperately wants to look "normal," he has significant anxiety that keeps him from being comfortable in any part of his life, whether at home or with friends or in school. As we can talk more openly about the anxiety, I can look for ways to be helpful, with both medication and with conversations in which he explores what makes him so anxious.

It is clear to me that a more directive sort of therapy, in which I asked questions or pushed Kyle to talk more about himself, would not have let us get to this point. He is very self-conscious about being "weird," about being anxious all the time, and he would have strongly resisted telling me much about it until he could be sure that my office, and the forty-five minutes with me twice weekly, was a safe place where he did not have to worry about being scolded or made fun of, and where his anxiety as well as his "tough guy" self could be accepted. He needs the time with me to be able to slowly be more comfortable with those parts of himself so that he can share them with me and let me help him understand how they connect to each other and to his depression.

Chapter 6

Friday

I start my day on Friday again at 8:00 a.m., but today I don't have an early appointment. There is no secretary until noon because Patty works ten hours four days a week so she can have a long weekend, and Darlene, my part-time secretary, comes in at noon. I start with checking messages on voice mail, checking the fax machine for incoming faxes, and turning on the coffee pot. Then I pull my charts for the day, finish notes I was not able to finish the previous day, and sit down with the computer to check emails and play a little solitaire.

At 9:00 a.m. I have an appointment with Mr. Abrams, a middle-aged man who has been in and out of therapy with me over at least twelve years. He first came to see me because of a significant depression. As we got to know each other, he let me know that he also has post-traumatic stress disorder and problems with holding on to close relationships. In our first sessions together he told me about his early history, which included significant abuse, loss of his only loving parent figure to cancer, and living on the street at age twelve (after he ran away from an abusive stepfather). As I listened, I could not stop myself from asking, "How did you survive?" Now, years later, he seems finally to be finding some stability in his life. He had another period of homelessness a few years ago, and we have together recognized a pattern in which he succeeds (wildly!) at a job, and then, in seven-year cycles, loses everything for reasons that seem to be (but probably are not completely) out of his control. In the last two years, he has returned for therapy and has continued to come consistently.

Dysfunctional Patterns Arising in Childhood

As we continue to talk, we have decided together that the cycle of success and then losing everything is repeating a seven-year cycle from his childhood. He lived with his loving adoptive mother until she died, and then with her husband, who became abusive. He ran away after seven years in that household. He spent the next seven years in various foster homes, sometimes living on the streets after running away again. What stability he had in those years came from two different foster homes with men who had strong moral cores and who did not put up with his defiance, but who were not abusive and gave him some control of his life. He believes that his ability to function and have some close relationships is directly because of what he learned from those men.

Mr. Abrams now can see the effect of his childhood trauma on his current life. He also sees that much of his current life is an attempt to repair some of that trauma. For instance, he is fiercely dedicated to the welfare of his grandchildren, their friends, and any other child he knows, trying to do for others what no one did for him. At the same time, he

140

avoids close relationships with just about everyone for fear of being hurt even more. He may be closer to me—whom he sees for forty-five minutes every two weeks—than almost anyone else; certainly he tells me things he doesn't tell anyone else. We both know that my willingness to let him run away when he needs, returning in six months or a year or two years without criticism, has allowed him to learn to trust me so that he can do the work to interrupt the seven-year cycle.

Mr. Abrams has missed several sessions. I prefer not to chase after people, trying to keep them in therapy when they want to leave, but I called him to remind him of today's appointment, hoping that he is not beginning another round of sabotaging himself. I did not push him to come in, but hoped that hearing from me would help him to remember what he wants to do with his life now. He does keep today's appointment, and he tells me he has spent several weeks just sitting in his apartment, feeling like there is no point in life. He says, "I didn't want to disappoint you, so I made it a point to make it here today. I didn't want to, though."

"Do you know what has changed? The last time I saw you, you were excited about your new job and about helping your son with his business."

"I don't know. Just all of a sudden I didn't want to even leave the house. I told Joe" (his son) "that he needed to handle this big job quickly because they won't put up with his being late. I had my own business for years, with big contracts all over, and I know what they need, but he doesn't want to listen to me."

"I'm remembering right now that a month or two ago you were talking about being with your grandkids, and how much you enjoyed playing with them and showing them how to tie their shoes and stuff. I know that it matters to you that you can help other people—especially your kids and grandkids. I wonder if having Joe not listen to you felt a little bit like you didn't have anything valuable to give him any more."

"*He* acts like he doesn't think I do."

"I think if you felt like you didn't have anything to give, you might pull back and feel like you were just worthless and might as well give up. That seems to be what sometimes starts the downhill slide in your seven-year cycles, and this kind of feels to me like what we've said about how they start for you."

"Maybe you're right. I don't know. . . ."

Patients Watching Us Closely

He goes on to say that for the most part he is doing pretty well, enjoying things with his grandchildren and resolving some ongoing practical issues (especially about money). He comments that I seem to be a little withdrawn myself, and wonders if I am feeling okay.

> I realize that he is watching very closely for hints about how I am feeling and what I am thinking: am I bored, am I pleased with him, am I emotionally available? Some of this watchfulness, for Mr. Abrams, is the hypervigilance that is a part of post-traumatic stress disorder. When your life depends on how other people are feeling, you become very skilled at finding clues to help you figure it out. Part of it, however, is what we see in all our patients. As we all know, and are specifically reminded by Casement and Maroda and others, our patients watch us very closely to make sure they know how we are feeling and to try to figure out what we are thinking. Today, I think, Mr. Abrams is checking to see if returning to the relationship with me is going

to hurt him (if I'm not in a good mood, not nice to him) or help him.

When he asks if I am okay, I laugh a little and say that I just haven't had enough coffee yet today; and he seems reassured that whatever may be going on with me is not about him. At the end of the hour, as he leaves he reassures me that he will be back the next week.

When Talking Isn't Enough

At 10:00 a.m. I see Ms. Buchanan, a middle-aged woman with a severe and treatment-resistant depression who has been seeing me for about fifteen years, and about whom I wrote in my first book. At first, she seemed to be the sort of patient who is the bread and butter of this work: depressed but functioning, coming regularly for weekly therapy and medication, and appearing to benefit from it. After several months of this sort of work with her, she unexpectedly began to be more and more depressed, to the point that she became unable to work. We tried most of the available antidepressant medications, got a second opinion about both medication and psychotherapy, and finally tried electroconvulsive therapy (shock treatment) as a last resort, but nothing was helpful. She continued to feel worse and worse and began to wish she were dead (although she was never actively suicidal). Throughout the medication trials and other therapies, we continued weekly psychotherapy, identifying and exploring her perfectionism and her habit of abandoning her own wishes so she could do what others expected or what was "right."

Finally, because nothing else was working, Ms. Buchanan agreed to try four-times-a-week psychoanalysis, but she could not tolerate lying on the couch unable to see me. She was never able to tell me why, but

I believe that without visual input she could not hold on to knowing emotionally that I was present in the room, and so she felt alone and abandoned. After only a week, Ms. Buchanan told me that she could not use the couch, and we agreed to begin a modified sort of art therapy, using play therapy techniques adapted to Ms. Buchanan's training as an art educator. She had become increasingly unable to tell me what was in her mind, so we started using painting to communicate. I would offer a prompt, such as "Paint what it's like when you're sad"; she would sit for a moment and then paint something in reaction to the prompt. She never quite seemed to feel that she was *deciding* to paint something in particular; rather, the paintings came as a sort of free association, bypassing her conscious intent.

For instance, early on I asked her to paint her depression. After a few seconds without speaking, she picked up a brush and the tube of black acrylic paint and produced a black rectangle, filled with black but with a red center. She finished, sat back, and was silent.

"Tell me about it," I said.

"It's a black box with a red center."

"What's the red?"

"I don't know."

"My reaction is to think it's anger, in the black of despair."

"That fits."

Early on, most of our exchanges followed this pattern. As we sat side-by-side, she would produce a painting and stop; I would inquire ("Tell me"); she would describe it concretely ("It's a black box" or "It's a cave with someone inside"). I would offer a response that included some emotion, and she would agree or demur. Usually there would be a piece of the description that I could ask about or use as another prompt ("Can you paint your anger?" "Who's the person in the cave?").

144

Within just a few weeks of this procedure, new things began to happen between Ms. Buchanan and me. Before, the emotional tone in the room had been flat, empty, and unconnected. Now, things felt alive, even though often not comfortable.

For a long time, Ms. Buchanan could still not talk about her emotions or thoughts. At times she sat silently, with tears falling, and when I inquired about the tears she could only say, "I don't know." As we continued with this work, she did begin to open up to some degree. There began to be slightly more spontaneity when she added details to her concrete descriptions. The early treatment is described in some detail in my first book, *Language and Connection in Psychotherapy: Words Matter.* Here I will jump to a time when Ms. Buchanan had painted a picture of herself in a pit, alone and desperate. I asked where I was in the picture, and she could not imagine that I might be willing to join her in the pit. Even the idea was confusing to her. When I asked her to paint that confusion, the picture was a woman in a fog of the colors that by now had come to represent confusion, anger, and fear, with eyes taped open and jangling noises at her ears.

As we sat and looked at this picture, I tried to imagine being the woman in the picture, and was distantly aware of feeling confused, overwhelmed, and frightened in that imagined self. I tried to find a way to manage the confusion: "What would it look like if the confusion was organized?" I expected a bland, unrevealing picture, with the same colors but not much else; and I thought the time it would take Ms. Buchanan to paint something would allow me to think of another potentially useful prompt.

What Ms. Buchanan did paint after a brief thought surprised me: it was a woman in war paint, with every element of the original picture converted into something protective. When I asked Ms. Buchanan to tell me about it, she said, "It makes me want to holler and yell ... go kick some ass." This was the first time she had reported feelings about a picture, not only content, and I was enormously excited.

This apparent breakthrough was short-lived, but over the next several months Ms. Buchanan was able to go back to the warrior woman, and together we found some of the strength and aliveness she had lost to her depression.

My work with Ms. Buchanan is not textbook psychoanalytic therapy, and is unusual enough that I spent a chapter describing and explaining it in my first book. In finding this intervention with Ms. Buchanan, I was heavily influenced by my training in child psychotherapy and child psychoanalysis because, with young children, the "talking cure" very often involves talking only when the conversation is part of play. The theoretical underpinning is the belief that anything that happens within the therapeutic hour is a communication of some sort, whether verbal or nonverbal, and that it is the job of the therapist to decipher that communication. In using Ms. Buchanan's art, I was able to find a way to help her communicate with me about her internal world even though initially she could not truly describe that internal world for herself.

Three-dimensional communication in art

Eventually the painting stopped being a useful gateway for Ms. Buchanan's unconscious communication, and there was another period of empty and unproductive sessions. I did not want to abandon the successful technique, and thought that perhaps three-dimensional art would be helpful, so I brought in some Play-Doh. With the Play-Doh

146

there was again a remarkable response, with some freeing up of Ms. Buchanan's ability to communicate. I began this time with a simple prompt, "What comes to mind?" Ms. Buchanan used the Play-Doh to make a lotus blossom ("Something beautiful out of the mucky dirt") and then a strip of land, and a plot began to emerge.

Ms. Buchanan made a seashore, saying that it was an island; a boat; and then another island with a boat wrecked on shore. She had a remarkable ability to create recognizable items from a few pieces of variously colored Play-Doh, and the story came alive.

The shipwreck dominated our time for several weeks. It was clear to both of us that Ms. Buchanan was the shipwreck victim, and I experienced despair and helplessness as I failed to find a way to shift the emerging narrative. After expressing what I understood as Ms. Buchanan's despair, I was able to be silent for several weeks, and she continued to be severely depressed, at times unable even to get out of bed and come to her sessions. We both felt shipwrecked, just like the Play-Doh castaway.

After approximately three weeks, during which she attended about half the scheduled sessions, Ms. Buchanan looked at the shipwreck scene, picked up the Play-Doh, and created a raft on which the castaway was able to get off the island. Then she created a scene with the castaway on the raft, meeting another boat with two people.

"Tell me about it."

"She's over the coral reef, and these two women rescued her."

"Who are they?"

"You and my acupuncturist."

The three women were seen on an island, where the Ms. Buchanan figure rested. After another two weeks, then, Ms. Buchanan left to explore the ocean, leaving me and the acupuncturist to rest on the island.

Dealing with Stalemates

After this hopeful interlude, the process again stalled, and the art was no longer useful for communication. Eventually, after a break in treatment for several months at Ms. Buchanan's request, we resumed our talk sessions. She now meets with me weekly for a double session (ninety minutes) of face-to-face therapy. Brief attempts over the last several years to resume the work with art have failed, and Ms. Buchanan clearly feels dissatisfied (but not completely shipwrecked) with her relationships and her life. She has unpredictable periods of time when she cannot even get out of bed for days at a time, and she is still not able to work, but she does have periods of time when she is able to find some things in her life to be content with. As I meet with her today, I am aware in the back of my mind of this long history in our work together, and I am alert and fully present, looking for ways to re-engage with her as productively as we have before.

> There is a risk with Ms. Buchanan, and with other long-term patients like her, that I will fall into a rut of being there but not really there: listening only to the surface of the conversation and not trying to identify the unconscious communications that can offer an opening to change. When I catch myself doing this, usually it is because there is something interfering with the feeling of connection and relatedness between us, as I said on Monday about Ms. Houghton and Ms. Gantman. With Ms. Buchanan, there have been no further periods when we were clearly finding new areas to explore, and it feels, in Ms. Buchanan's words, like she is saying the same old things every week.

Today she is doing what she often does, telling me what she did during the last week, with particular emphasis on the difficulties in two important relationships, the only close relationships she has now. She periodically wonders what she has done wrong, why the only friends she has are so oblivious to her needs. She can talk about her feelings now in ways she never could before, and is more able to experience some periods of peace and contentment, but she still feels isolated, alone, and lonely, struggling to connect emotionally with others.

> I have wondered at times if the therapy is truly helpful to her; but she declines to end the treatment or even to reduce the frequency, as if the connection with me is the only sustainable intimacy she has in her life.

Today she tells me she has been able to talk with her "boyfriend"—who lives in another state, whom she has not seen for several years, but to whom she stays connected online—about how angry and upset she sometimes gets with him. This week he has, unusually for him, listened and been responsive, and she feels good about being able to speak up to him.

She says, "I guess I *am* getting better at talking about my feelings. All these years when I'd come and just say the same old things over and over, it really did help. Without that I couldn't have gone this far. I guess it just took that long to get here!"

> There have been times in my practice when I felt as if I had a large number of patients who were "stalled," much like Ms. Buchanan had been: people who were chronically unhappy, usually significantly depressed, coming regularly for therapy

sessions and for medication reviews, but with both of us seemingly unable to find any traction in understanding them and their struggles. Some of them seemed to have what I think of as "neurobiological" issues, what some people call a "chemical imbalance": a disorder that clearly has its basis in the neurotransmitters in our nervous system, and for which medication is critical. Even those who clearly need medications usually also get at least a little relief from being listened to, but apparently not this group of people. When I find myself so stuck with these patients in their own particular hells, going nowhere and just feeling awful—in what I have named to myself as the "Slough of Despond"—I wonder what I have missed, what I am doing wrong, what I might do that might help. It is at these times that it is most tempting to change medications, or to give advice, to "do something." It is also at these times that I must most strongly remind myself that sometimes not knowing, and not doing anything except listening and waiting, is the appropriate response.

But how do we know when waiting is the appropriate response, and when it is in fact enabling, colluding with the patient's need to stay stuck? The simple answer is that we do not always know; and so we worry, and we talk with colleagues, and we imagine doing *something* that will make a difference. And finally, sometimes, the dam breaks: the waiting finally takes us to a place that offers some hope for change; or we think of something we haven't tried.

In thinking about how therapy works, at times I imagine it as if the patient and I are wandering in a dark wood. At the beginning of the treatment, we wander in the darkness, not knowing where we are going; at some point we have an insight about some part of the patient's life (I think of it as running into a tree), and we are able to put up a light on that tree in the woods. The light illuminates parts of the woods that we had not seen before, and so we can explore that for a while. Perhaps we have another insight that illuminates another patch of the forest; but eventually we come again to a dark place and must wander in the darkness again until we run into another tree. With Ms. Buchanan, we've been lost in the dark woods repeatedly for long periods, not finding any trees to allow putting up lights. The willingness to wander in that darkness, in the faith that eventually we will find a tree to put up a light, is what keeps me doing this work even when the patient and I are both stuck.

Discussion with Colleagues

After Ms. Buchanan leaves, I have a few moments to myself, and then I meet with Janet, Heidi, and two outside therapists for an informal group discussion. We call it "group supervision" because it began as my official supervision of Janet, Heidi, and Sandi, who also used to work for me. It has, over the years, slowly become more of a reading group: we meet and talk about our lives and interesting cases, and we read interesting articles. Recently we have been reading some of Winnicott's work, and today in our discussion we stumble onto a recognition that the practice currently has an unusually high number of patients whose central problems appear to revolve around issues of the false self/true self (Winnicott 1960): people who don't experience themselves as authentic or real, who don't know what they are "really" like, who go through life doing what's expected instead of what they want, who are seriously depressed and anxious because they can't find a way to "fit."

I'm puzzled by why there is such a grouping of patients with similar issues, and we all wonder whether reading Winnicott has made us more aware of those issues. It certainly is true that events in our daily lives affect what we notice in our patients because our unconscious running commentary and search for patterns—our reverie—is subtly shaped by those events. If I attend a conference on trauma, for instance, when I return to the office I will be more likely to recognize subtler signs of traumatic reactions, those I might otherwise miss. If one patient is exploring the ways in which the loss of his father in infancy affected his family and his life, I am more likely to think of issues of loss for other patients. When external events are striking, both my patients and I react: many years ago, the hospital where I was based was cutting down trees for a new building, and for several weeks, patients came in with dreams and associations about devastation, or war destroying the countryside. The trick is to recognize those outside influences, allow them free reign, but filter the associative stream of thoughts to find what is individually relevant to the patient in the office.

In our group discussion, the five of us can share some of these fragmented, incomplete thoughts and connections, and we can help each other fill them out to become useful pieces of our own professional selves, adding the ideas of others to our own. It helps us to take the theories we have studied and make them parts of our professional selves so that when we are in the room with our patients, we can simply use those thoughts and not have to step away from the emotional experience of the patient to access the theory. Someone along the way—I don't remember who—told me that theory does not belong in the room with the patient, even though we need theory in order to be in the room with the patient helpfully. As I said on Tuesday, in talking about Ms. Ma, I seldom think of theory when I am in the room with a patient, but I often think about it when talking with others about that patient, or when remembering the events of the hour, as I find a way to understand those events.

Embodying the Holding Environment

As the two-hour group discussion ends, we plan the reading and a date for the next month. After a short break, I go to greet Ms. Callahan, a young woman who came for treatment about a year earlier, saying that she was just not happy with her life but she didn't know why. We have spent our time together, on a weekly basis, exploring how she spends her time, what the relationships in her life are like, and the ways in which she tends to do what other people want instead of doing what she wants for fear of losing friends if she is "selfish." Today, as she walks in, she looks at the metal coyotes pacing on the bookcase and says, "Have those always been there?"

Surprised, I say "Yeah. Didn't you notice them before?"

"Not really. I guess I don't look much at things around me when I'm trying to be good." She looks around the office, and adds, "I guess most of this stuff is familiar, but I never really paid much attention to anything except you."

I have a sudden flash of memory of another patient who had asked if something was new in the office, and my surprise that people don't realize that nothing ever changes in my office space. For the most part, the furniture and the arrangement of the furniture have been the same for at least ten years, and I just take it for granted. It occurs to me that the ongoing sameness

153

is a part of what I try to offer my patients: the sameness of a place and a person that can take in their drama and their chaos and not be changed, that can be stable and solid even in the face of strong emotion. This is the physical embodiment of the "holding environment," the parent/therapist who can see the child/patient without falling apart or retaliating against anger or being overwhelmed, who can tolerate the patient's emotions and help the patient learn to tolerate and understand them.

Several years earlier I had re-upholstered the couch that my analytic patients use. It was very close to the color of the original fabric, but with a different pattern, and several of my patients were unsettled by that change for a few weeks until it became a part of the "sameness" that is containing and holding for both my patients and for me.

Ms. Callahan goes on to talk about her work that week, where she is becoming more assertive and more willing to call attention to her accomplishments. She is now being considered for a promotion and is anxious but excited about it. She adds that maybe she is noticing things more in her daily life as well as in my office, and she likes it.

A Late Cancellation

At two o'clock, I am again free; I had an appointment scheduled, but that patient called and cancelled because she was ill. She has missed a fair number of appointments lately, and I am concerned that she is on the verge of leaving her treatment; but I choose to deal with her about it in person at her next appointment.

As I think about her, I remember Langs's remarks about our patients using (or manipulating) reality to satisfy their unconscious wishes and fears, and I wonder what Ms. Callahan's unconscious wishes or fears might be.

Being real and containing real emotions

At 3:00 p.m., I have a phone appointment with Ms. Doakes. She is a middle-aged woman with post-traumatic stress disorder after an abusive marriage. She came into treatment with me shortly after she left her abusive husband, and has stayed through the divorce, losing custody of the children to the abusive husband (because of an inequitable court system in another state), a remarriage, and the birth of another child. She continues to struggle with occasional flashbacks and triggers when things such as particular numbers will remind her of events from her marriage. When Ms. Doakes remarried, she moved to another town; for a while I was able to see her in person weekly because I was consulting at a residential program near that community. Now, however, we have twice-weekly phone sessions because an attempt at Skype sessions, with visual contact, failed due to problems with internet connectivity. She has not been willing to find someone in her area to work with face-to-face, although I have encouraged her to do so, and she is quite vocal and articulate about why she wants to continue working with me. Today she tells me, "That's why I like you! You're not afraid to use real words, like bullshit or crap. Therapists need to walk through their patient's journey *with* them, and acknowledge it in real world terms; other therapists will say it's a 'challenging experience,' but you just say, 'That sucks!' I've been traumatized, and I need permission to express myself in real terms … I held it in for so long, and it nearly killed me. I didn't give myself permission to say, 'Oh, shit.' I just bottled it up and had all that junk that I couldn't get out.

"I need to express my feeling as a real person, not just textbook emotions. I've been dissociated so long, real words give me permission to be a real person, not all textbook-y. I don't feel them in my head, and I need to feel and process them … you've given me permission to do that."

I am somewhat taken aback by the flood of emotion, and just say, "Oh!" as she talks. She goes on, saying, "Too many therapists, it's like they're exploring this in a petri dish, and go home to their latte. You explore it like you're in the trenches with me, but you don't get caught. You give me a way to express my feelings, and you feel them without getting trapped with me. All my other therapists haven't been able to acknowledge things in a real way, a feeling way. Also with direction. You'll say, 'Maybe you can see it this way, there's another way to see that.' You always let me *first* get my own stuff out, barf it out all over the floor… My other therapists didn't let me barf it all out, they didn't listen. You let us talk, and spill our guts and cry and vomit it all out before you give *your* thoughts or opinions. You're very good at listening and understanding it all … and you don't talk down to us or condescend to us."

Although I am surprised at the outburst, it does seem to me that Ms. Doakes is expressing what I try to do: to allow people to tell me what is real to them, in a way that makes it real to both of us; and then to help them find ways to think about it that can contain the emotional pain and make sense of it so they can go on with their lives. I am often uncomfortable when patients tell me what a wonderful therapist I am; I think I am good at what I do, but I am very aware that I do sometimes make mistakes, or fail to do what I want, and that there is always someone who is better than me. I have learned over the years that it is important, however, to accept what feels to me like idealization by my patients. If I cannot acknowledge that I am good, and good for them, they may react by going to the other extreme, feeling that I am useless and worthless, and it gives them a reason to escape from the hard work. If I can admit that I know I am good at what I do, but still remind both of us that sometimes I make mistakes, we can work together to find what is right for them, not just what I think is right but what they also think is right. It also, of course, makes it easier for me to persist in the work when I know it is appreciated and is good work.

Modifying the Frame to Meet the Patient

After talking with Ms. Doakes, I take a minute to step back from that experience and regain my equilibrium before I speak with Mr. Edgeworth. This is also a telephone session, with a middle-aged man who came to me for symptoms related to military service as well as to a difficult childhood and several failed marriages. When he took a job out of the area, he also did not want to see anyone else because he has difficulty with trusting people and had come to trust me with his history and with his feelings. I have not insisted on maintaining a rigid frame in his treatment, and it is essentially an "on demand" sort of therapy. When we speak he may say that he has nothing to talk about and will end the session after five or ten minutes. Other days, he will use the entire time. I often wonder if I am doing him a service by relaxing the frame, but he appears to use it well. When he has difficult issues in his life, either at work or with his family, he will talk to me about it; he thinks about his dreams, and sometimes he will bring me a dream with a ready-made interpretation of what it means, asking if I have other ideas about it. Over the years that we have had this somewhat piecemeal

157

treatment going, he has found some peace and has made a good life for himself with a wife and child. He frequently finds new things about his own childhood that he remembers and can sort through with me, allowing him to be a better father to his own son and a better husband to his current wife.

> My training tells me that the slow surfacing of new memories and new insights is the best evidence that what we are doing is working. I also know that when I have tried to insist on more regular sessions, with a more traditional pattern of work, he has either dropped out of treatment for several months or has simply not been able to comply. Perhaps my willingness to accommodate this pattern is, as Langs says (see Wednesday), my ignorance or my countertransference interfering with appropriate management of this acting out of a resistance. Or perhaps, as Winnicott would suggest (again, see the Wednesday discussion on the frame), Mr. Edgeworth is one of those individuals who require a "specialised environmental provision" in order to be able to work at all.

Mr. Edgeworth has told me that he sees me as a mother figure, and often will say, "Since my mother was no good, I need someone like you to help me better myself. I need you to tell me when I'm being stupid, like Grandpa would have." Grandfather, the only supportive adult in Mr. Edgeworth's life, died a few years ago, and I have been given his emotional place in Mr. Edgeworth's internal world.

> At this point, I have decided that I agree with Winnicott and, as long as Mr. Edgeworth continues to show slow progress in being able to rely on his own decision-making, it is acceptable to

allow the maternal idealization and not insist on changing how we work. I do continue to think about how I will know when it is time to step back and metaphorically push Mr. Edgeworth out of the maternal nest.

Evolution of Clinical Presentation

My last appointment on Friday is another Skype session, with Frank, a twenty-one-year old man who has been in on-and-off treatment with me since he was about age ten. Early on he had a significant anxiety disorder and was struggling in school because of the anxiety about being around so many other people. He tends to manage his anxiety by obsessive-compulsive actions; he controls his environment with compulsive neatness and compulsive handwashing as a way of managing the anxiety about what bad things might happen if he is not in control. We spent perhaps a year in individual psychotherapy, with medication for the anxiety, and he seemed to be doing well.

Frank is very bright, and in high school he worked hard to do everything he needed to do and to make good grades. There were some conflicts with school personnel, especially when he felt unable to attend gym because of his anxiety about possible germs, but for the most part he managed relatively well. In his junior year, however, he began to be unable to make himself complete his work, and he returned for psychotherapy about that struggle. It was enlightening to see the change in this young man. From being a frightened boy, who had seemed very vulnerable and needed lots of support and reassurance, he has become—at least to superficial acquaintance—a self-assured, somewhat angry, and controlling young man. He thought that when other people disagreed with him they were of course wrong; he attributed his difficulty with school (especially English) to not seeing the point of doing things that he already knew how to do. He wanted just to move on and get his college diploma so he could go into the work he had chosen.

If I had not known Frank early in his life, I would have accepted the apparently controlling and angry personality as the most important part of his personality. He managed to hide his anxiety, even from himself for the most part, so that he didn't have to feel vulnerable in any way. He could admit that he worried about politics, and generally felt that the people who are running the country are doing a bad job; but he talked about those issues with a great deal of contempt and scorn rather than letting his fear of the future emerge to be seen and felt. In general, he tried not to talk or think about fears or worries that came closer to home, and he was quite successful in presenting himself to others as more angry or irritated than as anxious.

Over the last three years, Frank and I have met regularly to try to help him find ways of accomplishing what he wants to do with his life in the face of his inexplicable inability to actually do the work that he needs to do as the first steps in his career path. The idea that he needs to stop complaining about how stupid it is, and just do the homework and get it over with, was so foreign to him that he was unable to comply with the requirements of the school system for a regular high school diploma.

We had regular exchanges in which he asserted the complete irrelevance of poetry to his life plans. I would remind him that state law requires English for a high school diploma, and suggest that perhaps something about the emotions evoked by poetry made him uncomfortable. He always adamantly denied that poetry evoked any feeling in him.

I was quite sure in my own mind that Frank was unable to bring himself to do his schoolwork because he was avoiding something that made him uncomfortable, but I could not seem to find a way "in" to help him recognize what he was avoiding.

Enactments

After trying a period of cyber school—during which he was not able to log on regularly because he didn't see the point of the routine of the classes—Frank dropped out of high school and completed a GED, which allowed him to enter college. In his first two years of college, he continued to struggle with classes. He was able to push himself to do the English and other "gen ed" classes required, but now he had problems with an advanced math class required for his chosen major.

> I have struggled for some months to figure out exactly what is interfering with Frank's ability to use his formidable intelligence in school. Finally, I decided tentatively that Frank does not recognize that there is anything in life that has any meaning other than its surface meaning: "feelings" to him are "just a collection of behaviors" that can be listed and then dismissed. In math, he believes that going to lectures, doing the assignments, and reading the book should be enough to learn the work. He has not been able to apply what he has learned in lectures and reading to practical problems unless they are problems that he has seen before: that is, he has learned the "collection of behaviors" that allows him to solve problems that he has seen solved, but he cannot apply overall principles to find new approaches to new problems, and so he cannot practically use the material he has memorized. Although this feels to me like it fits, it also does not feel like it really explains the enormous trouble Frank has had.

His difficulty clearly is an internal psychological problem, not purely an academic one: in one class, he was about to pass when he managed to fail it entirely because he "mistook" the date that the final exam was due (what we call a Freudian slip).

In recent sessions, I have started to notice that Frank and I are in some ways caught in an "enactment," a repetition between us of patterns of behavior from the past. In psychoanalytic theory, an enactment is a pattern of nonverbal interactions between therapist and patient that serves unconscious functions for both. What I have realized is that Frank is doing what he did in middle school: going through the motions of working on a problem, while in truth he is waiting for the authority figure to fix the problem.

In middle school, he spent hours "negotiating" with the school guidance counselor about why he couldn't go to gym because he couldn't touch the dirty sports equipment. Eventually he agreed that if he could wear gloves he would go; and then he refused to actually go. Through his public school years, school authorities made numerous accommodations to allow Frank to complete his high school diploma before he finally sidestepped the requirements altogether by getting a GED.

With me, Frank is also going through the motions in the therapy—keeping appointments, answering questions—but contributing few of his own thoughts to the discourse in the belief that the answer will emerge if he goes through the motions. This is in some ways similar to what Mr. Ignatz was doing in his trust that if he just said whatever came to mind and trusted the process, things would change (see Tuesday). Mr. Ignatz, however, was able to say what came to his own mind, while Frank waits for *me* to decide what to discuss. He is waiting patiently (or stubbornly?) for me to find an answer for him rather than working *with* me to explore his thoughts and feelings (which he dismisses as unimportant) about the problems he is having. I have had extraordinary difficulty in explaining to Frank why his feelings do matter and why just listening to my remarks and questions without his active contributions will not lead us to any helpful answers. It appears that the concept of "insight," as something that can make it possible to do things you couldn't do before, is foreign to him.

Today I am trying to explain this pattern to him: that he is doing with me what he did in science class, doing the exercises but not really *using* the concepts that he has memorized, so that it is not helping him to address new or unfamiliar problems. I fall into what has become a familiar pattern of almost scolding him, trying to force him to recognize what is so obvious to me: that he cannot live his life without recognizing his feelings and addressing them. As usual, we end the session after forty-five minutes with me feeling frustrated and stuck. I challenge Frank to tell me in the next session what *he* wants to get out of our time together, hoping that this will start him thinking about his own ideas, not mine.

As the session ends, I recognize belatedly what has again happened; and this time it occurs to me that perhaps the countertransference/transference enactment—the repetition between Frank and myself of old patterns of behavior—is what happened when he was in middle school: he essentially refuses to do what is needed, and waits for the "adult" to find some way to make it unnecessary for him to do what he does not want to do. I also remember with chagrin that transference-countertransference enactments like this do not only express the patient's issues; and I remember what I had temporarily forgotten: that if I am working harder than my patient, I am being driven by my countertransference need to "change" things instead of allowing the patient to do what *he* needs.

An enactment is a behavior that becomes current in the *actions* between therapist and patient, not only in memory and feelings but because it also expresses some important conflict of the therapist. So I must reflect on what in me is responding to Frank's behavior with such irritation. I finally conclude that my anger at Frank is because I was always the good girl who wanted to rebel against the expectations of school, society, parents ... but never had the courage. I am perhaps jealous that he is willing to take the risks I avoided, and I am concerned about what he might lose in taking those risks—almost as if the loss would be my own.

I still am not sure how to eventually deal with it with Frank, but at least I have found some footing that might allow for a more productive approach than just scolding (after all, if lecturing worked, he wouldn't need to be in my office!). Recognizing the enactment, and in particular recognizing my own contribution to it, will help me avoid repeating the pattern yet again and find another way to intervene.

I go home with that hope of getting unstuck with Frank next week, and anticipating the end of my workweek on Saturday.

Chapter 7

Saturday

Saturday is a short day. I have always worked Saturday mornings because I grew up in a family where both parents worked in my father's office Saturday mornings; and when I was in high school I also worked at the office. It just seems right to me not to take that time off. Since opening my practice, I have also found that many people are grateful for the Saturday time and for evening hours so that they can come regularly for sessions without having to miss work. Adolescents sometimes balk at getting up early on Saturday for a therapy session, but if they have most weekday afternoons filled with soccer or band practice or other extracurricular activities, they may prefer Saturday morning anyway.

I begin the day as usual, checking messages, checking for faxes, pulling charts, making coffee. On Saturday, I have no secretary until about 11:00 a.m. The building door is locked (as it is in the evenings) so

I must be sure the phone rings in my consulting room, allowing me to let people into the building when they buzz up from the outside door. Saturdays feel slower to me since there are usually no messages and most of the paperwork for the week is done. If I have notes unfinished, I will try to get them done before I leave for the day, and I will try to clear my desk of things undone.

Planning to End

At 8:00 a.m., Georgia comes in: she is a young woman who falls into the group of "false self" patients that we talked about in the group discussion on Friday. She came into treatment in high school, complaining of significant depression and inability to make herself do most of the things she wanted (or was expected) to do, including go to school. She was cutting herself superficially and said that cutting made her feel "more real," as if the pain and seeing the blood reminded her that she truly existed. In twice weekly psychotherapy for several years, she was able to learn enough about herself that she no longer feels "not real," and she has not cut herself for at least a year. She has, however, become significantly rebellious, and she experiments with doing what *she* wants to do instead of what her parents and the rest of the world expect her to do. She has bright green streaks in her hair, dresses in a Goth style with boots and a leather collar, and seems to want to outrage as many people as she can in this somewhat conservative community. She does, however, have an impish sense of humor, and is able to laugh at herself about her need to outrage others. She is currently working as a server at a local restaurant but plans eventually to go back to school (once she has proven to her parents, and to herself, that it is for *herself*, not because *they* want her to).

166

Today we are talking about perhaps ending the treatment, as she feels much more comfortable in her life and in her ability to plan for the future successfully. She says with some anxiety that she would like to be able to come back if she starts to have problems again. I tell her that of course she can come back whenever she wants. At the end of the session we agree that we will meet monthly for another six months, giving us time to talk about what it feels like to be independent from me as well as from her parents, and she leaves with a smile to go to work.

New Psychoanalytic Case

At 9:00 a.m., I meet with Ms. Harrison, a middle-aged woman who recently moved to the area from another state and asked specifically to see me about psychoanalysis. She has some awareness about the difference between other therapies, such as cognitive behavioral therapy and analytic psychotherapy, and between psychotherapy and formal psychoanalysis. Ms. Harrison has had two previous episodes of depression that were treated with medication and CBT, and she says now that she doesn't want to try that approach again: "I don't want to just put on rose-colored glasses."

CBT, a widely practiced form of therapy, is action and behavior oriented. As I described it in the Introduction, it assumes that a person's mood is directly related to his or her patterns of thought, and CBT interventions focus on helping people to change how they think. For many people, CBT is very helpful and can offer lasting improvement; but for Ms. Harrison clearly there is something going on in her daily functioning that changing thought patterns does not address. This is the sort of patient for whom psychoanalysis is highly appropriate, and sometimes nothing less intense can help. She is psychologically minded, has some insight into past problems with relationships that contribute to her depression, and seems quite able to tolerate the intensity of the emotions that will likely be brought to the fore in her treatment. I suspect that her transference to me (the feelings about the therapist that are repetitions of past patterns of relatedness with important figures) will be a negative paternal transference: she will likely see me as powerful and negative in some ways, much as she saw her father in her childhood, and this will complicate the treatment because she will want to "fight back" when she feels threatened by me. We tentatively agree to start with twice a week therapy for two months because I cannot find time in my schedule for a four times a week frequency until later. In those two months, we will be able to confirm her capacity to tolerate the work without falling apart, and we should be able to establish a fairly solid therapeutic alliance that will help us negotiate the rocky shoals of a negative transference. We also talk about a fee that is affordable to her, which is less than my usual hourly fee (as I usually will do for more frequent sessions to keep therapy affordable) but enough that I will not resent the reduction in income.

As Ms. Harrison leaves, I am excited about the opportunity to have a new psychoanalytic case. Including her I will have four patients in formal psychoanalysis (Ms. Austin, Mr. Ignatz, Ms. Harrison, and my next patient, Mr. Ibbetson). Most analysts at this time are not able to have a full analytic practice so fill out their schedules with psychotherapy cases. Thus four is quite a respectable number, especially in a community unfamiliar with psychoanalysis.

Weekend Crust

At 10:00 a.m. I see Mr. Ibbetson, a middle-aged man who generally comes four times a week (but this week was out of town). He is a blue-collar worker who supplements his income with side jobs as an artist, and he spends much of his time trying to find ways to feel comfortable in his daily life. He usually feels that he is never good enough, is intensely aware of his lack of formal training in his art (although he is quite talented), and often feels criticized by others. Over the eight years he has been in treatment, he has become aware of how his self-criticism and the expectation of criticism by others repeat what he felt as a child. He struggles to allow himself to feel more confident and to remember that not everyone is like his family was. Today he talks about being surprised that he was okay during the two weeks that we have not met (due to first my vacation and then his own). He had expected to feel lost and abandoned, but apparently was able to enjoy himself without particular difficulty.

> As I listen, I wonder if this is evidence that Mr. Ibbetson may be ready to end his treatment. Prior to the break in the treatment, he had cancelled several appointments for pleasure trips with friends; and he has lately been talking a lot about other things in his life ending. Perhaps these are signs that he is ready to end. I do not bring up the subject today, since we are re-establishing the relationship after the break. For now, I will simply bear it in mind, and when it occurs to me again, I will ask him what he thinks about the possibility. I will need to be a little careful about how I bring it up because he has a tendency to see similar questions as signs that I want to get rid of him; but I believe he may be ready to think about it over the next few months.

I am aware with Mr. Ibbetson today of what analysts sometimes call the "weekend crust," although we see it any time there is a break in the flow of the therapy, not only after weekends. Because psychoanalysis is usually four or five sessions in a row, each day the patient comes back slightly less defended: that is, slightly more able to acknowledge and talk about the issues that are uncomfortable and are therefore avoided by forgetting or disguising or changing the subject. Throughout the week the patient becomes able to explore deeper and deeper material. By the last session of the week, often we are able to talk about issues that would otherwise stir up very strong emotions, issues that cannot be reached on Monday. With the weekend break of several days, and with interruptions due to missed appointments or vacations, the important and painful material goes back into hiding: the defenses are again strong enough to prevent conscious awareness of the material, and in the first sessions of the week those defenses once again will be seen, will be pointed out to the patient, and will slowly lessen, allowing the difficult material to come up again. In this way, very slowly over time, we are able to get past the layers of avoidance and denial so that the patient can ultimately allow himself to know more what thoughts and feelings are leading him to the behaviors that he wants to change in his life. With Mr. Ibbetson today, the "crust" is apparent, but relatively "thin" because he is well along in his treatment, and so the defenses are not as strong.

A Final Session

My 11:00 a.m. appointment is also someone whose treatment is going well, so I am feeling very positive and hopeful as I end my week. Mr. Johnson is a middle-aged man who came to me after a bitter divorce for help with his depression at the loss of that relationship. As we talked about his grief and anger at the divorce, he made an offhand remark that he was "feeling more suicidal than he was comfortable with." I was taken aback at the idea that feeling suicidal could be "comfortable," and inquired about what he meant, only to find that he had wanted to die off and on since his childhood, and had thought it was just "one of those things that people deal with." As we explored why he wanted to die, and what his life has been like over the years, it became clear that he had always expected to lose loved ones. He grew up in a neighborhood in New York City that was filled with Holocaust survivors, and the prevailing tone of his environment was one of loss and grief and despair. In our work together over several years, he has found a connection to the positives in his life, has found things to be hopeful about, and no longer expects to be abandoned by everyone. He has been able to establish a new, loving relationship with a woman whom he wants to marry, and has let go of his anger at his ex-wife so they are able to be civil to each other. We have been talking for some months about ending the therapy, and Mr. Johnson feels he is ready (as long as he knows that he can come back if he needs). He leaves at the end of the hour with a final good-bye and hope for his future.

When I say good-bye to Mr. Johnson, Darlene, my part-time secretary, has come in. She will stay for several hours, filing all the paperwork that has been generated over the course of the week and balancing the checkbook. I finish my notes for the week, clear off the desk, and leave with the same feeling of "rightness" that started the week:

I am doing what I want to be doing with my life, and I am making a difference in the world.

Final Thoughts

We have finished the week now and are coming to the end of this book, and I have been reflecting on how writing it has changed me. When I began writing, I knew a lot about how I worked, and believed that it would be relatively easy to explain it to others. As I wrote, I was reminded of what I know intellectually but usually don't dwell on: everything I do has multiple reasons.

Reasons

Some of what I do comes from my choice of treatment modality, professional training, and experience, such as paying attention to a patient's life history and not just the current symptom. Some of it is because it is easier from a practical sense to do things one way than another, such as having almost all the patients in my office speak to one of the therapists before speaking with me. And some of what I do comes out of my own individual psychological and emotional makeup: my preference to do psychotherapy rather than exclusively medication monitoring, as many physicians do, is in part because of my curiosity and my wish to get to know a small number of people very well rather than a large number of people superficially.

Being able to explain clearly the reasons for how I work, and to distinguish what I have learned in training and experience from what I do because of personal preference and practicality, has required that I look more closely at how I work than I have for many years. I now consistently think more deeply about why I do things the way I do, and why I say what I say to my patients. I more often do with myself what I do with my patients: I do not take anything at face value but look below the surface, and I think about how I think.

Rules

Thinking about how my patients think—as a colleague says, "holding the other person's mind in mind"—and thinking about how I think is an important part of this work, perhaps the most important part of the work. As I have thought more deeply about what I do, I have noticed some things for the first time. For instance, I had not noticed how much of what I do can be seen as nontraditional, as breaking the "rules" of psychotherapy. I have always felt that I was just doing what made sense, what the patients required for their own work in therapy, and did not see it as particularly unusual. Writing about how and why I practice differently than I was taught has pushed me to consider why I am comfortable with being less traditional. I value the classical ways of practicing psychoanalysis and psychotherapy, and am clear about some of the negative consequences of departing from that classical practice. In describing how I actually do practice, I have realized that although I break the "rules" of psychotherapy fairly often, I do not violate the underlying reasons for those rules. For instance, the teaching about not taking gifts is to make sure we do not take advantage of our patients; as

I deal with each individual about his or her wish to give me a gift, I try always to handle it in the way that best meets his or her emotional needs.

Therapeutic Stance and Timelessness

I have also noticed a pattern about how I enter into the therapeutic relationship in each session. A few weeks ago I was sitting in the front office, chatting with Janet, when my next patient came into the waiting room. I said hello and immediately followed the patient down the hall to my consulting room, leaving the conversation with Janet. As I entered the consulting room, I was aware of a shift in my internal state. From being social, relaxed, and joking about current events, I fell reflexively into the neutral stance, an "even-handed, nonjudgmental interest" (Alvarez 1985) in the inner life and motives of my patient, so that I could offer the holding space in which my patient could be whoever she needed to be. I took the step into the psychic space that belongs to the patient, the state-dependent memory of the patient that I talked about in Thursday's discussion of supervision.

Later that day, I thought about that reflexive step into a way of being that is very different from how I am outside the office. I believe that reflexive step explains the comment of one of the early readers of this book: that it seems to have no beginning, middle, or end. The person who told me that believed it was a problem, but I don't think it is. My life certainly had a beginning, and will have an end, and right now I am (more or less) in the middle of it; but I don't experience it that way. I experience it as the *now*, and I don't worry too much about the beginning or the end except in early memories or in actions like making wills. That's also how I experience my work: with each patient, I keep in mind the beginning of the work, the many beginnings and endings of each session, and the end that will eventually come, but I experience each moment as the *now*.

The step into neutrality and into the "now" of a particular session is a step into an essentially timeless way of being. The psychoanalytic process is simultaneously both timeless and time-bound. It is timeless because of the sameness and because the analyst ideally is available for as long as the patient needs to keep coming for treatment. Our conversations together take place in the timelessness of the unconscious, where events from our early childhood still affect us when we are in our forties or fifties or sixties. It is time-bound because each session ends and the patient has to leave; but the patient and the analyst each know that the patient is coming back, and the unfinished thoughts can be finished tomorrow or next week or next year. The timelessness is important because our unconscious conflicts cannot just be summoned up at our command; they must be coaxed and unearthed slowly. The time-boundedness is important because it is important sometimes to interrupt the conversation, to let the issue "simmer" in our mutual unconsciouses, to see what comes up for the next time. The interruption of the process by the end of the hour is a part of the process, allowing the patient (and the analyst) to stay grounded in everyday life. Without that interruption, that built-in distance from the emotion of the material, we might be consumed by it, swallowed up and unable to observe it and reflect on it so we can use it to change.

Good-byes

The interruption of the process by the end of the hour also compels the patient to face the reality of loss in everyday life. Each session is a hello at the beginning of the hour, and a good-bye at the end of the hour. For patients who struggle with not being able to tolerate good-byes, or who struggle with loss, even that temporary good-bye can be painful. Many of the anecdotes that therapists pass around among themselves have to do with "doorway moments"—when patients wait until the last five seconds of the hour to say something that is critically important—or with ways in which patients manage to come late or stay past the end of the hour, or somehow make the good-byes less painful. The question of time and how much time is enough is addressed at some point in almost every analytic treatment. We end the session because time is up, not because we have solved the problem at hand; and that reminder that the problem still exists keeps us grounded. We also end the therapy because the patient is ready to move on independently, not because the problem that brought them in is gone. Mr. Johnson, for example, who ended his treatment on Saturday, will always be sensitive to loss and to good-byes, but he could leave because he was ready to manage that sensitivity within himself without becoming depressed and suicidal again.

Like almost everything in this work, the timelessness of psychoanalysis is both a strength, a foundational element of the work, and a weakness, a potential block to the work. When we approach an hour with the intent to wait to see what comes up, it can be very easy to fall into drifting from day to day, from session to session, forgetting that the patient has a life outside of the analytic consulting room, and that our task is to help them be more comfortable and more effective in their lives away from us. The repeated good-byes, with sessions ending, with vacations, with the coming and going from the therapeutic relationship, helps to keep the therapy from becoming endless and pointless.

It is of course not only patients who struggle with good-byes and who sometimes have trouble letting go. The relationships with my patients are important to me, and when I say good-bye to Mr. Johnson, or to Georgia, and when I consider whether Mr. Ibbetson is ready to leave his analysis, I am aware of both the sadness of loss and the pleasure of a job well done. My work as a therapist is aimed toward making it possible for the patient to not need me, to be able to inhabit life fully and not have to deny the painful parts of life. When that goal is achieved, then I have an obligation myself to accept the painful good-bye and let go. The end of the hour, and the end of the therapy, are ways that we assert our separateness and allow our patients to be their own person.

Good-byes happen in different ways in psychoanalytic therapy. Sometimes we can hear patients moving toward saying that they want to end therapy, and we identify the wish and explore it. Sometimes they can't tell us they want to go, and they just cancel appointments until it is obvious. Then again we identify the wish and help them to explore it. Sometimes they just go, missing appointments and not rescheduling and not giving us a chance to work it through with them. Ultimately, the treatment ends because the patient stops coming, not because there are no issues left to work on.

In all these cases, we try to find a way to sit with the reality of loss and accept it, to not try to hold on, but to surrender our own wishes to the needs of the patient. Over and over, we notice that when we can surrender in this way, when we stop holding on and just accept that the patient is leaving, something opens up between us, and they can then tell us why they need to leave; or they remember why they don't want to leave, and the therapy moves to a deeper level. As with our patients, when we can accept the loss, it makes room to think about new things.

I find myself having some of the same trouble letting go of this book. There is so much more to say, and so much more to know, that I want to keep going and to say everything I have learned in a lifetime of listening and learning to know others. But there is a rhythm to what we can do, and sometimes we have to just let go and let the incompleteness be enough.

Final Points

As we approach the end of the book, I want to lay out clearly some of the points that are particularly important. I have illustrated each of them throughout the description of this week in my professional life, but they are worth repeating.

Trust the Process

First of all, in my work I ground myself in the belief that whatever issues bring my patients to therapy, their unconscious knows what they need. If I can stay with the process and provide the neutral space that allows them to find themselves, they will get there. I believe that everyone has an innate impulse toward emotional health; it is possible to find it when we can get our unconscious conflicts out of the way. A part of helping to move those unconscious conflicts out of the way takes place, in psychotherapy, as we shake up the psychological "order" that the patient came in with, allowing temporary internal chaos and disorganization in order to open the opportunity for change. The patient's impulse toward emotional health will then reorganize that chaos in a way that works better for her/him than the previous way of being.

Remember the Elements of Therapy

Second, the elements of therapy always include holding, containing, and mirroring. Holding involves providing the neutral space, with the nonintrusive therapist, so the patient can look for and find his or her true self instead of complying with the expectations of others (including the therapist) in a false-self adaptation to society. Without that holding, nothing lasting happens.

Containing means that we live with the fear and grief and rage—and any other feelings—that come with letting go of unrealistic wishes.

179

The goal is to find ways to live in life as it is, not as we want it to be, and to change what we can change but to accept what we can't change. Tolerating the craziness or the anger within ourselves and others, and getting through it to find the joy that is also a part of life, is how we contain the therapy and the patient.

Mirroring is recognizing in the patient, and helping the patient to recognize, the true self that comes out of the disorganization and chaos, the reorganization that allows us to live with the world-as-it-is, instead of the world-as-we-want-it-to-be or the world-as-we-are-afraid-it-is. Ultimately my goal for all my patients is to help them to know themselves better and to inhabit themselves fully, to help them learn not to deny the painful parts of themselves.

In the process of holding and containing and mirroring, we have to do some of the same things for ourselves. To do this work, I need to have a space in my life where I can be myself so I can find my balance as I contain the intense emotions that my patients and I experience in our work together. The "holding environment" of my office is a holding environment not only for my patients, but also for myself, with the sense of peace and lack of intrusion from the outside world that holding provides. The containment is provided by discussion with colleagues when I have particularly thorny situations to deal with and by reading and refreshing my grounding in the theory of my work, as well as by knowing myself as fully as I can so as to contain my own internal conflicts. The mirroring—recognizing myself as valuable—also comes in discussions with colleagues and in seeing improvement in my patients and hearing from them that they appreciate the work. Writing this book and sharing what I have learned in my years of practice has served to mirror me to myself because I have been able to step back and recognize more clearly what I do and how I do it.

Don't Take Sides

One of the more difficult things to remember in this work is that everything we do is multidetermined: there is never only one meaning for a behavior and never only one reason. One of my early supervisors used to say that for an analyst, the appropriate response to a multiple-choice question is always "All of the above" because most often all the reasons we can imagine for a particular behavior are at least partly true. The art of the work lies in finding which of the possible meanings of the patient's behavior is *most* true while remembering that the other possible meanings also matter and must be addressed. Not infrequently, I find that the easiest way to discover alternate meanings of a particular behavior is to consider the polar opposite of what seems to be the most significant element. True neutrality involves focusing not only on one side of the question, but considering all.

Mind the Transference

I also want to stress the importance of the transference. In psychoanalysis proper, consideration of the transference is the central technique that helps to move the treatment forward; in psychoanalytic psychotherapy, the transference is a central element but not *the* central element. In nonanalytic therapies, the transference often is not considered at all. I find it hard to imagine being able to understand how someone functions in the world without considering transference (which is not limited to psychotherapeutic interactions). In every relationship, we react to others based on our past experiences with people: almost everyone, for instance, feels at least a little guilty at the beginning of a traffic stop because we all have had experiences as children of misbehaving and getting into trouble with authority figures. That is transference in everyday life.

As a colleague told me years ago, the best source of history about a particular patient's past is the transference: the ways in which the patient responds to me will tell me about what important relationships in his life were like. I may not know initially if the critical figure was mother or father or someone else, but I know that there was some important someone who was critical, and that the patient expects others to treat him or her as that person did. Paying attention to the transference, and helping the patient learn to pay attention to it, opens many doors to understanding.

And finally, the process begun in the consulting room goes on after the patient leaves us. In analytic psychotherapy, as in so many parts of life, the journey is more important than the destination: the process is what matters. That is part of the timelessness of psychoanalysis because the process never stops. I had some trouble deciding how to end this book because it began a process for me that I suspect will not stop in my lifetime. So perhaps I'll just say, as I do at the end of each session, "We have to stop now."

Acknowledgements

There are so many people who deserve my gratitude for their contributions to my work and to this book that I had trouble deciding where to start; so I will just list them in random order and in groups:

My family, who showed me what a "facilitating environment" truly is. My parents taught me to love learning and reading, and my sisters have continued to encourage my writing.

The staff at my office who provide the containment that makes my work possible. Janet and Heidi, the therapists in the office, share the work and the thinking about it; Patty and Darlene and Lisa, my secretarial staff, truly are "support" staff, and I could not continue without them to take care of administrative issues so I can think about patients.

My writing group at New Directions: Writing with a Psychoanalytic Edge, at the Washington-Baltimore Center for Psychoanalysis. Kate Daniels, Sharon Alperovitz, Kaja Weeks, and Joan Turkus have been with me since the beginnings of this book, both praising and criticizing, and the book has its final shape in large part because of their input. Hattie Myers and Joanna Goodman have joined us in the last year, adding their encouragement and support. As we discuss our writing, they reflect me back to myself, and show me how I am reflected in my writing.

And of course always my patients, who have been willing to share their lives with me and from whom I have learned everything I told you in this book.

References

Ainsworth, M. D. S., Blehar, M. D., Waters E., and Wall S. 1978. *Patterns of Attachment: A Psychological Study of the Strange Situation.* Hillsdale, NJ: Erlbaum.

Alford, F. C. 2016. *Trauma, Culture, and PTSD.* College Park, MD: Palgrave Macmillan.

Alvarez, A. 1985. "The Problem of Neutrality." *Journal of Child Psychotherapy* 11, no. 1: 87–103. https://doi.org/10.1080/00754178508254765.

Bacal, H. A., and Thomson, P. 1998. "Optimal Responsiveness and the Therapist's Reaction to the Patient's Unresponsiveness." In *Optimal Responsiveness: How Therapists Heal Their Patients*, edited by H. A. Bacal, 249–270. Northvale, NJ: Jason Aronson.

Bion, W. R. 1962. *Learning from Experience.* London: Tavistock.

Bion, W. 1967. "Notes on Memory and Desire." *Psychoanalytic Forum* 2, no. 3: 271–286.

Blagys, M. D., and Hilsenroth, M. J. 2000. "Distinctive Features of Short-Term Psychodynamic-Interpersonal Psychotherapy: A Review of the Comparative Psychotherapy Process Literature." *Clinical Psychology: Science and Practice* 7, no. 2: 167–188.

Borgogno, F., and Fortune, C. 2008. "Notes and Fragment of a Psychoanalytic Vocation. Interview of Franco Borgogno by

Christopher Fortune." *American Journal of Psychoanalysis* 68, no. 1: 69–94.

Casement, P. 1991. *Learning from the Patient.* New York: Guilford Press.

Casement, P. 2002. *Learning from Our Mistakes: Beyond Dogma in Psychoanalysis and Psychotherapy.* New York: Guilford Press.

Clarkin, J. F., Levy, K. N., Lenzenweger, M. F., and Kernberg, O. F. 2007. "Evaluating Three Treatments for Borderline Personality Disorder: A Multiwave Study." *American Journal of Psychiatry* 164, no. 6 (June): 922–928.

Davis, M. 2012. *Language and Communication in Psychotherapy: Words Matter.* New York: Jason Aronson.

De Maat, S., De Jonghe, F., Schoevers, R., and Dekker, J. 2009. "The Effectiveness of Long Term Psychoanalytic Psychotherapy: A Systemic Review of Empirical Studies." *Harvard Review of Psychiatry* 17, no. 1: 1–23. https://doi.org/10.1080/10673220902742476.

Freedman N., Hoffenberg J. D., Vorus N., and Frosch, A. 1999. "The Effectiveness of Psychoanalytic Psychotherapy: The Role of Treatment Duration, Frequency of Sessions, and the Therapeutic Relationship." *Journal of the American Psychoanalytic Association* 47, no. 3: 741–42.

Freud, S. 1901. *The Psychopathology of Everyday Life.* Translated by A.A. Brill. London: Hogarth Press.

Freud, S. 1937. "Analysis Terminable and Interminable." *International Journal of Psycho-Analysis* 18: 373–405.

Hopkins, L. 2006. *False Self: The Life of Masud Khan.* New York: Other Press.

Kernberg, O. F., Yeomans, F. E., Clarkin, J. F., and Levy, K. N. 2008. "Transference Focused Psychotherapy: Overview and Update." *International Journal of Psychoanalysis* 89, no. 3: 601–620.

Langs, R. 1981. *The Technique of Psychoanalytic Psychotherapy*, Vol. 1. Northvale, NJ: Jason Aronson

Leichsenring, F. 2005. "Are Psychodynamic and Psychoanalytic Therapies Effective? A Review of Empirical Data." *International Journal of Psychoanalysis* 86, no. 3: 841–68.

Maroda, K. 2004. *The Power of Countertransference: Innovations in Analytic Technique*. Hillsdale, NJ: The Analytic Press.

Maroda, K. 2005. "Legitimate Gratification of the Analyst's Needs." *Contemporary Psychoanalysis* 41, no. 3: 371–388.

Masur, C. 2018. "Depression: A Psychoanalytic Perspective." In *Psychoanalytic Trends in Theory and Practice*, edited by Etezady, M. H., Blom, I., and Davis, M. Lanham, MD: Lexington Books.

Mitchell, S. 1997. *Influence and Autonomy in Psychoanalysis*. Hillsdale, NJ: The Analytic Press.

Ogden, T. H. 2002. *Reverie and Interpretation: Sensing Something Human*. London: Karnac Books.

Rodman, F. R., ed. 1987. *The Spontaneous Gesture: Selected Letters of D. W. Winnicott*. Cambridge, MA: Harvard University Press.

Smith, J. M. 2012. *An Absorbing Errand: How Artists and Craftsmen Make Their Way to Mastery*. Berkeley, CA: Counterpoint.

Sullivan, H. S. 1953. *Conceptions of Modern Psychiatry: The First Williamson Alanson White Memorial Lecture*. New York: W. W. Norton & Company, Ltd.

Winnicott, D. W. 1960. "The Theory of the Parent-Infant Relationship." *The International Journal of Psychoanalysis* 41: 585–595.

Winnicott, D. W. 1965a. "The Capacity to Be Alone." In *The Maturational Processes and the Facilitating Environment*, 29–36. London: Hogarth Press and the Institute of Psycho-Analysis.

Winnicott, D. W. 1965b. "Communicating and Not Communicating Leading to a Study of Certain Opposites." In *The Maturational*

Processes and the Facilitating Environment, 179–192. London: Hogarth Press and the Institute of Psycho-Analysis.

Winnicott, D. W. 1965c. "Ego Distortion in Terms of True and False Self." In *The Maturational Processes and the Facilitating Environment*, 140–152. London: Hogarth Press and the Institute of Psycho-Analysis.

Winnicott, D. W. 1989a. "The Importance of the Setting in Meeting Regression in Psycho-Analysis." In *Psychoanalytic Explorations*, edited by Winnicott, Clare, Shepherd, Ray, and Davis, Madeleine, 101. Cambridge, MA: Harvard University Press.

Winnicott, D. W. 1989b. "Two Notes on the Use of Silence." In *Psychoanalytic Explorations*, edited by Winnicott, Clare, Shepherd, Ray, and Davis, Madeleine, 85. Cambridge, MA: Harvard University Press.